Reg

DrawPlus 8 User Guide

How to Contact Us

Our main office (UK, Europe):

The Software Centre
PO Box 2000, Nottingham, NG11 7GW, UK

Main	(0115) 914 2000
Registration (UK only)	(0800) 376 1989
Sales (UK only)	(0800) 376 7070
Technical Support (UK only)	(0845) 345 6770
Customer Service (UK only)	(0845) 345 6770
Customer Service/ Technical Support (International)	+44 115 914 9090
General Fax	(0115) 914 2020
Technical Support e-mail	**support@serif.co.uk**

American office (USA, Canada):

The Software Center
13 Columbia Drive, Suite 5, Amherst, NH 03031

Main	(603) 889-8650
Registration	(800) 794-6876
Sales	(800) 55-SERIF or 557-3743
Technical Support	(603) 886-6642
Customer Service	(800) 489-6720
General Fax	(603) 889-1127
Technical Support e-mail	**support@serif.com**

Online

Visit us on the Web at	**http://www.serif.com**
Serif newsgroups	**news://news.serif.com**

International

Please contact your local distributor/dealer. For further details please contact us at one of our phone numbers above.

Comments or other feedback

We want to hear from you! Please e-mail **feedback@serif.com** with your ideas and comments, or use the Serif Web forums!

Contents

1
Welcome

Introduction

Welcome to DrawPlus 8.0 and the remarkable power of vector graphics—the complete drawing, graphics and illustration solution for your home, school, church, or growing business. DrawPlus 8.0 can "do it all" for you—or let you do it all yourself, with total control over its versatile drawing features.

Whether you're meeting DrawPlus for the first time or have been with it through many versions, you're sure to appreciate the combination of high performance, fair price, and ease of use. In fact, it makes so many things so easy to do, you might just think about retiring that paint program you've been using!

About this User Guide

Read this guide to learn how to install, start and use DrawPlus 8.0, from the basics to tips and tricks for advanced users. Here's a brief chapter summary:

1. **Welcome**. How to install and start DrawPlus and an overview of key features.
2. **Getting Started**. A quick look at the DrawPlus user interface and an introduction to creating new or opening existing drawings with and without the Startup Wizard.
3. **Working with Objects**. A hands-on overview to help you become "object-oriented."
4. **Lines, Curves and Shapes**. An in-depth look at creating and editing figures built up from line objects.
5. **Brushes**. How to apply an artist's brush via a mouse or pen tablet.
6. **QuickShapes, Connectors, Text, and Pictures**. How to create and edit these essential DrawPlus objects.
7. **Fill, Line, and Transparency Effects**. Introduces the concepts and tools you'll need to create spectacular results.
8. **Using Layout Tools**. A tour of basic and advanced control features that can help you work accurately and efficiently.
9. **Special Effects**. A host of additional effects tools to enhance your creativity, with design examples.
10. **Animation and Web Graphics**. How to produce animations and web graphics.
11. **Exporting and Publishing**. A look at exporting graphics for the web, and desktop and professional printing (via PDF).

About DrawPlus 8.0

DrawPlus 8.0 not only offers an electronic drawing solution which breaks the price-performance barrier but provides a feature-rich design environment for expressing your creativity!

Without further ado, let's look at the new and established features that make up DrawPlus 8.0.

What's new in DrawPlus 8.0

- **Brushes** (p. 83)
  Unleash the painter within you, with DrawPlus's powerful new **Paintbrush Tool** and supporting brush galleries! Nearly 200 vector- and Bitmap-based brush types are at your disposal—pick from acrylic, watercolour, pastel, paint and charcoal categories, or create your own categories.

  Interested in creating your own brushes? Convert any DrawPlus object to a vector brush with a single click or create bitmap-based brushes in a unique **Brush Edit** dialog. Alternatively, you can edit any brush preset at any time. Import your digital photos to create Picture brushes with ease.

  Using a pressure-sensitive pen tablet (**Serif GraphicsPad** or equivalent)? Pressure sensitivity is supported with preset or custom pressure profiles and control over the maximum and minimum pressure applied. Additionally, scale the brush stroke's width and opacity with pressure. Pressure sensitivity is simulated when applying brush strokes with your mouse.

- **Paper textures** (p. 34)
  Apply a paper texture (**Canvas, Cartridge**, **Embossed**, **Parchment**, and **Watercolour**) to layer-specific objects—give a textured look to any artwork. Perfect as a complement to your final composition!

- **Open PDFs with Ease** (p. 30)
  Unlock the contents of third-party PDF drawings using DrawPlus's impressive "open PDF" feature—objects can be brought into a new drawing with a single-click for immediate editing.

- **Onboard Image adjustments** (p. 118)
  Benefit from image adjustments for quick colour correction of imported images (and objects converted to pictures)—pick from automatic adjustments (**Auto Levels**, **Auto Contrast**) and manual adjustments (**Brightness/Contrast**, **Channel Mixer**, **Dust and Scratch Remover**) to name but a few. Commonly used special effects such as **Diffuse Glow**, **Shadows&Highlights**, and various blurs make up the set of adjustments, which can be applied in combination. You can now eliminate the dreaded red eye effect on subjects in your imported pictures with the new single-click **Red Eye Tool**. Benefit from improved importing of pictures from **Photoshop .PSD files**.

- **A New Graphical Interface** (p. 26)
  The much changed user interface of DrawPlus benefits from a greater focus on tool accessibility, workspace management of toolbars and tabs (for maximized workspace area), and a more modern experience for design work. The remodelled Studio tabs are now dockable, and can additionally be collapsed, grouped or resized in any combination or direction. New tabs include **Swatches**, **Layers**, **Transform**, **Align**, and the powerful double act, the **Brushes** and **Pressure** tabs. Create different configurations of these tabs and save them as separate workspaces for instant recall whenever you wish!

- **Design Templates** (p. 28)
  Why start from an empty page? Instead, use DrawPlus's always-at-hand collection of commonly used designs (Greeting Cards, Invitations, Letterheads) you've been asking for. For technical drawings, take advantage of design templates based on ISO/ANSI standards.

- **DrawPlus Templates** (p. 32)
  If you would like to reuse your design, simply save your drawing as a **DrawPlus Template (.DPX)**. Any new drawing can then be based on your saved template, which is made easily available via the Startup Wizard's **start from scratch** option.

- **Gallery Tab** (p. 34)
  The Gallery tab provides an impressive selection of instantly available ShapeArt, SymbolArt, Home design symbols, and various other connecting symbols for family trees, electronics, computers, and many more. Use the Gallery to additionally store and organize your own favourite designs for future use!

- **Context Toolbars** (p. 27)
  DrawPlus now supports context toolbars which host tool options and settings that dynamically change according to the currently selected object or tool used in your drawing. Only the necessary tool settings and options are at hand for edit or reference, speeding up the design process while making the user experience easier.

- **Colour mixer** (p. 127)
  Choose from different colour mixing modes in the Colour tab—**HSL Wheel**, **HSL Square**, **RGB Sliders** or **CMYK Sliders** all offer different ways to mix colour. The HSL Wheel mode offers intuitive colour mixing based on colour selection from a Hue wheel, then associated Saturation and Lightness levels from a triangle. Additionally, apply shading/tinting with the Colour tab's **Tinting** feature.

- **Object Default control** (p. 60)
  Set your intended object's default line colour/style, fill, and transparency before even drawing your object! As a more powerful default control, **Synchronize Defaults** let's you adopt a currently selected object's attributes for future objects; For example, select a red brush stroke, to subsequently paint in red, then a green brush stroke to paint in green; all or only selected attributes can be affected. Global and object-specific defaults can be reset independently.

- **New Colour Palettes** (p. 128)
  Load RGB, CMYK or coordinated "themed" palettes from within the Swatches tab. Add, view, edit or delete colours used in your current drawing from within a **Document Palette**, which can be saved for use in subsequent drawings. Create you own palettes at any time.

- **Linked Colours** (p. 129)
  With DrawPlus, you can define new colour sets based on a base colour. This linkage can transform the drawing's colour scheme instantly, by simply modifying that base colour. Try this out on your Gallery tab's room and garden layouts.

- **PDF Printing for Professionals** (p. 224)
  PDF export to the PDF/X-1 or PDF/X-1a file format is a great choice for professional output from DrawPlus. Deliver with confidence to your print partner, safe in the knowledge that your single composite print-ready PDF drawing includes all fonts and colour information for spot or process colour separation. Select file information, crop marks, registration targets, and densitometer/colour calibration bars for inclusion in your PDF.

- **..and some very useful improvements you've been asking for!** Opening saved work now provides Folder and History views for intuitive navigation. **Import AutoCad® files** (.DXF/.DWG; including AutoCad 2006®) directly. For improved layout, you can change the grid colour and style (dots, dashes and lines). Use grid lines for precision drawing of room layouts or engineering/scientific projects. Snap to guides or grid independently. Tired of ungrouping complex groups to edit an individual object?—use the **Ctrl** key with object selection. Need **foreign language support**? Simply paste text in Unicode format as either formatted RTF or unformatted plain text. **Vector clipping** of multiple objects completes the latest improvements.

Plus these established features...

- **Multipage Document Support**
  From startup to printout, the versatile DrawPlus engine sustains your creativity. Choose from a wide range of **preset document types**, including **booklets** and **folded documents**. Work on pages right side up... **automatic imposition** assures correct order and orientation of your output.

- **Total Ease-of-Use**
  You'll find accelerated learning tools like ToolTips, and context-sensitive Hints & Tips. The tabbed Studio—storing hundreds of preset lines, fills, transparencies, and design elements—is always convenient and ready to use. Especially for working at high zoom levels, the Navigator tab affords a thumbnail of your entire drawing with the visible area shown as a draggable view box.

- **Text Inside Shapes**
  Simply create a shape, then type into it! New **shape text** flows to fit the containing object for unlimited layout possibilities. Great for flowcharts and family trees!

- **QuickShapes**
  Can't draw? Won't draw? QuickShapes are the answer! They work like intelligent clipart… or the most powerful set of drawing tools you've ever envisaged. Even extremely complex shapes like spirals, stars, and webs are simple to draw and customize using QuickShapes. QuickShapes will also take text as with freeform shapes.

- **Enhanced Text Handling**
  Edit shape text or standard (free) text right on the page... apply basic formatting from the always-on-hand **Text context toolbar**. Control advanced properties like text flow (wrap), kerning, leading, paragraph indents, above/below spacing.

- **Professional-Standard Drawing Features**
  Features like converting text to curves, defining custom envelopes, fully customizable drop shadows, layers, and scalable vector graphics give complete creative power. Plus special commands like Contour for outlining and edge effects... Add to composite two shapes into one... Subtract for cropping and masking... Intersect to carve out unique shapes and regions. With our Autotrace converter, bring paint-type art into DrawPlus in fully editable vector format.

- **Design Power with Colour Gradient Fills**
  The Gradient Fill Editor allows you to adjust gradient contour and tint **any portion** of the colour spread, **locate key colours** precisely... and select from **RGB**, **HSL**, **CMYK**, **PANTONE®** or **Registration** colours via a Colour Selector dialog.

- **Advanced Fill Support**
  Apply high-end linear, radial, conical, ellipse, Three Colour, Four Colour, Square, and Plasma fills to any text or shape for exciting, professional results. Simply apply solid colours from the Studio's Colour or Swatches tab onto a fill path to add or replace colours for more subtle gradients. Use Bitmap fills—with over 250 supplied bitmap images in a range of categories for textures and backgrounds. Even import your own bitmaps and use them as fills on DrawPlus objects! Plus Mesh Fills for impressively varied gradients using a path-node network.

- **Transparency Effects**
  Transparency can make the difference between flat, ordinary visuals and sparkling realism! And DrawPlus provides it all—a full range of transparencies for shading, shadows, reflections, depth effects, and more.

- **Versatile Line Drawing**
  Sketch using **calligraphic lines** with an adjustable pen angle. Add **rounded corners** when and where you need them. Create and save your own line styles using customizable dot and dash patterns... and choose different end caps and joins.

- **Chain Lines**
  Here's the ultimate in decorative line effects: easy to apply from the scores of pre-supplied choices, just as easy to edit or create from scratch! Chains take drawn objects and link them in sequence along a designated line, for marching footprints, themed borders, and much more.

- **Dimension Lines and Scale Setting**
  Click a couple of times to take linear or angular measurements of any object on the page—DrawPlus displays the dimension using your choice of ruler units, at your specified scale (say, one inch to two feet). Dimensions update when objects are moved or resized! Design room layouts, make maps, draw scale models... the choice is yours.

- **Connectors**
  For drawing dynamic flow diagrams, schematics, family trees, and organization charts, connector objects let you link your boxes and symbols and then rearrange at will. Connection points stay put on each object... keeping connections intact. Auto Connectors intelligently display bridges at line crossings, and even route themselves around obstructive objects.

- **Natural Curve Editing**
  Simply click and drag to break and redraw a curve at any node. Apply smoothing selectively to freeform curves to eliminate that "shaky hand" appearance.

- **Intelligent Curve Tracing**
  Now simply "connect the dots" to trace around curved objects and pictures... the Pen Tool features **Smart segments** that use automatic curve-fitting to connect each node!

- **Animation Mode**
  Tap the power of QuickShapes to turn out Web animations in no time—using advanced features like onion skinning, backgrounds, overlays, and frame management.

- **Web Image Slices, Hotspots, Rollover States**
  Beat the pros at their own game by using these techniques to add links to your Web graphics! With a few clicks, divide images into segments — each with its own hyperlink and popup text—or add hotspots to specific regions. Even let DrawPlus create rollover graphics that highlight or change state when users mouse over or click!

- **Web Browser Preview**
  One click lets you see how your graphics will display in a Web browser, so you can quickly check quality, transparency, hyperlinks, and rollover behaviour prior to final export.

- **Filter Effects**
  Drop shadows starting to wear a bit thin? Enliven your text with fully adjustable Inner Shadow, Glow, Bevel, and Emboss filters... easy to apply and sure to impress. Apply soft edges with the **Feathering** filter effect—great for blends, montages, vignetted photo borders, and much more.

- **Dramatic Dimensionality**
  Why settle for only two dimensions? **Instant 3D** adds realistic depth to ordinary objects and text. Use one master control panel to vary extrusion, rotation, bevel, lighting, texture, render and more.

- **Astounding 3D Lighting and Surface Effects**
  Advanced algorithms bring flat shapes to life! Choose one or more effects, then vary surface and source light properties. Start with a pattern or a function, adjust parameters for incredible surface contours, textures, fills. The Studio's **Effects** tab offers preset 3D effects you can apply and customize as you wish.

- **Perspective Effects**
  Get a new slant on things... With a selection of context toolbar presets plus a built-in tool for freeform adjustments, the **Perspective Tool** lets you tilt and skew text (or any other object) for truly "spatial" results!

- **Cropping**
  Any object can serve as a "cookie cutter" for trimming one or more other objects into a single shape... and the effect is reversible so you won't lose your originals. Great for creating "reflections" of complex scenes!

- **Roughen Tool**
  For jagged, jaunty edges on text, lines, or QuickShapes, just drag the tool up or down for subtle or bold results.

- **Border Wizard**
  The vastly flexible Border Wizard instantly adds borders to the page or to individual objects. Choose a border from the extensive library, or be creative and let Border Wizard guide you through building a unique design.

- **Image Export Optimizer**
  The Export Optimizer lets you see how your image will look (and how much space it will take up) before you save it! Its multi-window display provides side-by-side WYSIWYG previews of image quality at various output settings, so you can make the best choice every time.

- **PDF (Portable Document Format) Export**
  Step up to the worldwide standard for cross-platform, WYSIWYG electronic information delivery. Your **PDF output** will look just like your DrawPlus document... in one compact package with embeddable fonts, easily printable or viewable in a Web browser.

- **Professional Print Output**
  Artwork can be prepared for professional printing straight from DrawPlus. Spot or process colour (CMYK) separations for full colour printing are possible. You have full control over prepress settings for output.

Registration, Upgrades, and Support

If you see the Registration Wizard when you launch DrawPlus, please take a moment to complete the registration process. Just call Serif free phone and provide the installation number and code shown. We'll give you a personalized registration number in return. Remember, if you need technical support please contact us. We aim to provide fast, friendly service and knowledgeable help.

Installation

What you need to run DrawPlus 8.0

If you need help installing Windows, or setting up peripherals, see Windows documentation and help.

Minimum:

- IBM compatible Pentium PC with CD-ROM drive and mouse (or other Microsoft compatible pointing device)
- Microsoft Windows® 98 SE, Me, 2000, or XP operating system
- 32MB RAM (Windows 98 SE), see manufacturer's requirements for other operating systems
- 205MB (recommended full install) free hard disk space
- SVGA (800x600, 16-bit colour) display or higher.

Additional disk resources and memory are required when editing large or complex documents.

To enjoy the full benefit of brushes and their textures, you must be using a computer whose processor supports SSE. On brush selection, an onscreen message will indicate if your computer is non-SSE.

Optional:

- Windows-compatible printer
- TWAIN-compatible scanner and/or digital camera
- Pressure-sensitive pen tablet (**Serif GraphicsPad** or equivalent)
- Internet account and connection required for accessing online resources

First-time install

To install DrawPlus 8.0 simply insert the DrawPlus 8.0 Program CD-ROM into your CD-ROM drive. The AutoRun feature automatically starts the Setup process. (If it doesn't, follow the manual install procedure described below.) Just answer the on-screen questions to install the program.

DrawPlus 8.0 Resource CD-ROM

If you also have the DrawPlus 8.0 Resource CD-ROM, it's a good idea to install that as soon as you've finished installing from the DrawPlus 8.0 Program CD-ROM. Again, the AutoRun feature will automatically start the Setup when the Resource CD-ROM is inserted into your CD-ROM drive.

Manual install/re-install

To re-install the software or to change the installation at a later date, select **Settings/Control Panel** from the Windows Start menu and then click on the **Add/Remove Programs** icon. Make sure the DrawPlus 8.0 Program CD-ROM is inserted into your CD-ROM drive, click the **Install...** button and then simply follow the on-screen instructions.

2
Getting Started

Once DrawPlus has been installed you're all ready to go! Setup adds a **Serif DrawPlus 8** icon to the **Programs** group of the Windows **Start** menu.

Click the Windows **Start** button to launch DrawPlus. If DrawPlus is already running, choose **New>New from Startup Wizard...** from the File menu.

DrawPlus Startup Wizard

The Startup Wizard appears whenever you start DrawPlus and presents you with five choices.

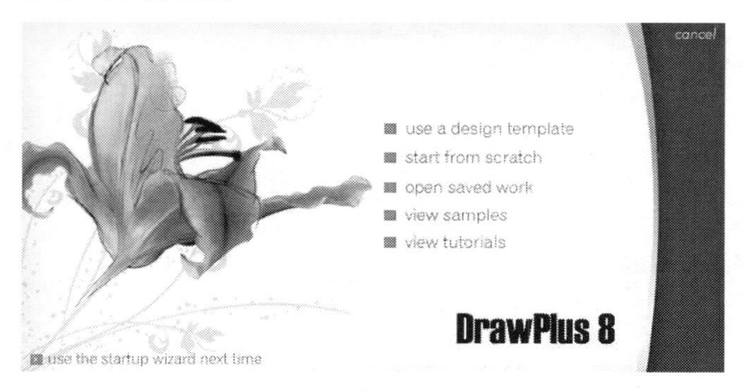

- **use a design template**, to create an instant drawing from a design
- **start from scratch**, to create a new drawing
- **open saved work**, to open and edit your saved DrawPlus drawing files
- **view samples**, to load some example drawing files to boost the imagination!
- **view tutorials**, to access the DrawPlus tutorials (more available on DrawPlus 8 Resource CD-ROM)

To quickly see a new drawing, based on DrawPlus's defaults, select **cancel** in the top-right corner of the Startup Wizard.

The User Interface

Let's take a moment to look at the key parts of the DrawPlus interface. The top menu bar hosts various menus offering an alternative to accessing toolbars or tabs; less commonly used commands are also present.

File Edit View Insert Format Tools Arrange Window Help

The toolbars and tabs in DrawPlus are as follows:

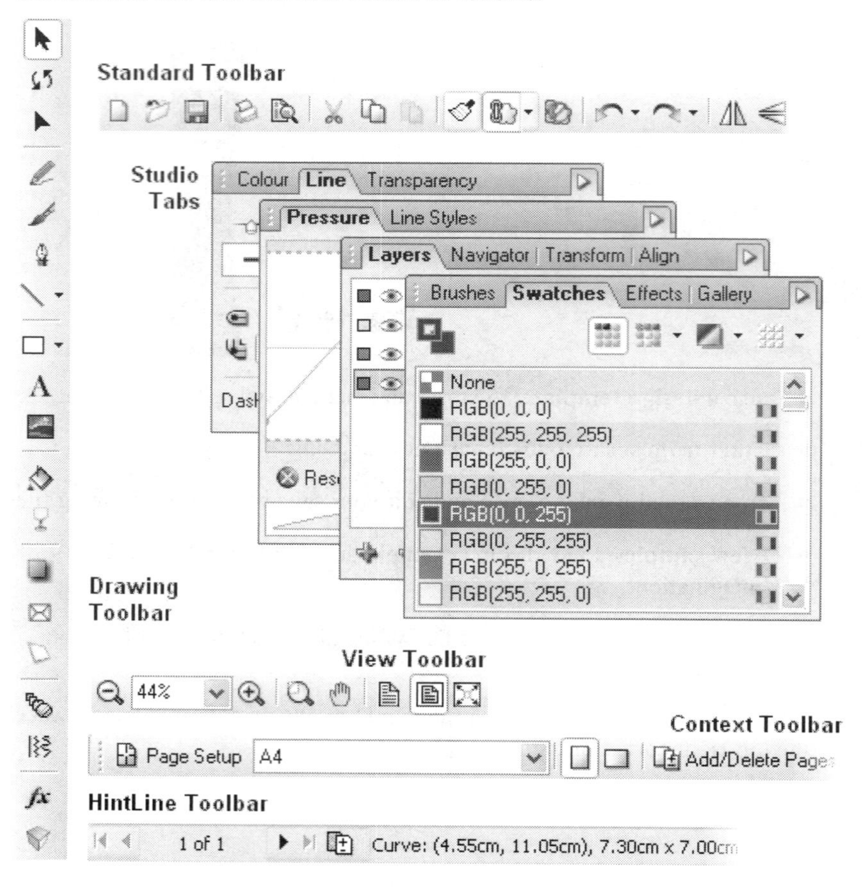

- DrawPlus tools are arranged in menus, toolbars (Standard, Drawing, View, Context, Web (not shown) and HintLine), and tabs contained in the **Studio** area on the right side of the screen.

- The **Context** toolbar changes dynamically with the type of object or tool currently selected—only the necessary tool settings and options are shown for edit or reference.

- At the bottom of the workspace you'll see the **HintLine** toolbar readout. As you move the mouse pointer over menu items, toolbar buttons, and tab controls, you'll see popup ToolTips or capsule descriptions of each feature appear in the HintLine.

- To access online help and resources, you can choose **DrawPlus Help** from the Help menu at any time (or press **F1**). The main help screen includes a table of contents and the Visual Reference, which lets you browse interface elements—simply click an item for details. Click the **Index** tab for an alphabetical list of terms and topics, or **Search** for free text searching.

The active area of the DrawPlus display is made up of two areas, the **page** and the surrounding **pasteboard** area. You can draw onto either area but it is the page area that will be printed. You can use the pasteboard to store items that you might want to use in a design or to experiment with them.

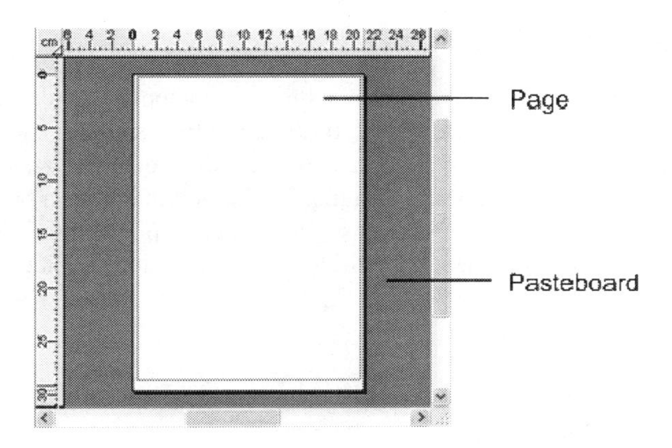

Creating drawings from Design Templates

It's so much easier creating drawings with a little bit of help—DrawPlus can utilize a whole range of design templates which will speed you through the creation of all types of drawings!

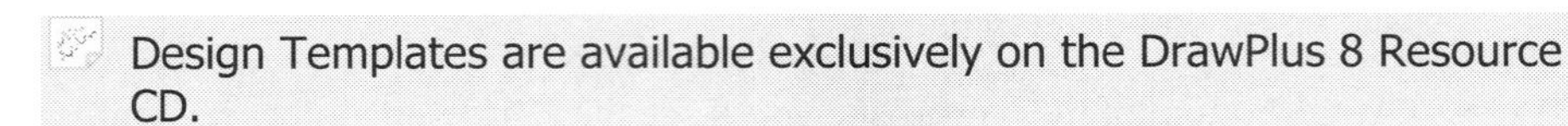
Design Templates are available exclusively on the DrawPlus 8 Resource CD.

To create a drawing from a design template:

1. Launch DrawPlus, or choose **New>New from Startup Wizard...** from the File menu.
2. Click **use a design template**. You'll be prompted to select a category and can then choose from a wide range of design options.
3. Select a drawing category on the left, and examine the samples on the right. Click the sample that's closest to what you want, then click **Finish**.

The above method is the only way to access Design Templates. If you've switched the Startup Wizard off (and don't see it when you start up), you can switch it on again. Choose **Options...** from the Tools menu and check **Startup Wizard** on the **Ease of Use** pane.

Starting from Scratch

Perhaps the greatest thing about DrawPlus is the way it supports your creative efforts, but doesn't supplant your own creativity. DrawPlus samples can serve as useful starting points for creative work; they may save you a few steps or inspire you to produce more personal designs. But behind them lies a powerful document-formatting engine which affords a vast range of possibilities. You can choose from various document categories, with illustrations depicting preset document types, i.e.

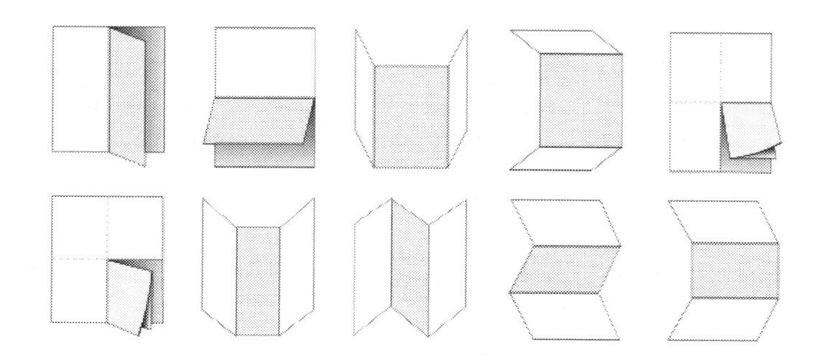

To create a new drawing using Startup Wizard:

1. Start DrawPlus (or choose **File>New>New from Startup Wizard...** if it's already running).
2. Select **start from scratch** from the Startup Wizard.
3. Select a document category from the Documents pane. Categories contain preset document types (see above) or if you select **Regular**, you can choose from standard document sizes presented in Portrait or Landscape sub-categories. For custom sized pages, choose the **Custom Page Setup** button.
4. Select a document type and click **Open**. The new document opens as a single blank page.

The **My Templates** category let's you base your new drawing on a previously saved template.

To create a new drawing during your DrawPlus session:

1. Choose **New>New Drawing** from the File menu, or enter **Ctrl-N**.
   OR
2. Click the **New** button on the Standard toolbar (if Startup Wizard is disabled).

You'll get a new drawing in a new untitled window each time you choose this method—the default page size is adopted.

You can always adjust the page size and document format later via the **File>Page Setup...** dialog.

Take a moment to check the ruler markings along the top and left of the workspace. User Guide examples will usually show centimetres—but you can set any ruler unit you prefer. Simply choose **Options** from the Tools menu, select the **Layout** pane, and pick a unit from the “Ruler Units” list.

We’ll look at Rulers, Guides and Snapping in the Positioning Aids section on p. 163.

Opening an Existing Drawing

You can open an existing DrawPlus drawing either from the Startup Wizard, Standard toolbar or the File menu.

To open an existing document from the Startup Wizard:

1. Select the **open saved work** option. In the Documents pane of the **Open Saved Work** dialog, you'll see either your computer's folder structure for navigation to your DrawPlus drawings (Folders tab) or a list of most recently used drawings (History tab). Preview thumbnails can be shown in the adjacent pane.
2. Select a file name or sample, then click **Open**.

To open an existing drawing via tool bar or menu:

1. Click the **Open** button on the Standard toolbar, or select **File>Open...**.
2. In the Open dialog, navigate to, then select the file name and click the **Open** button.

Opening PDFs

It is possible to open any PDF document (created with DrawPlus or other applications) in DrawPlus—you can save the PDF file as a DrawPlus Drawing (.DPP). The character formatting, layout and images in the original PDF document are preserved to allow comprehensive editing of the document.

DrawPlus attempts to display all text, objects and graphics on a best effort basis. The diversity and complexity of PDF file contents, from a myriad of original sources, may mean that opening the PDF cannot be guaranteed to display every page element successfully. A warning message "*DrawPlus found <n> features that it didn't understand in the file*" is displayed if elements of an opened PDF document cannot be interpreted—this may or may not result in visible errors in your drawing after opening. It is suggested that the PDF contents are visibly checked if a warning message is generated on opening.

To open a PDF file:

1. Select **File>Open**.
2. Select the name of the file, and click the **Open** button. The PDF document is opened and will repaginate to the number of pages of the original PDF document.
3. Use **Save** or **Save As...** in the File menu to save as a DrawPlus Drawing (*.DPP). The file name is by default based on the original PDF file name but this can be edited as required.

Your opened PDF file will still be named as a .PDF file in your title bar until you perform a **Save** or **Save As....**

Opening AutoCad files

DrawPlus opens AutoCad® .DWG and .DXF files quickly and easily. Using the same process as that for PDF files, this creates an opportunity to not only view engineering layouts and designs (up to AutoCad 2006) in DrawPlus, but to edit the drawn objects and to save the drawing as a DrawPlus Drawing (.DPP).

On file open, a dialog provides options to scale the Autocad file objects, position the artwork on the page and merge objects onto one layer.

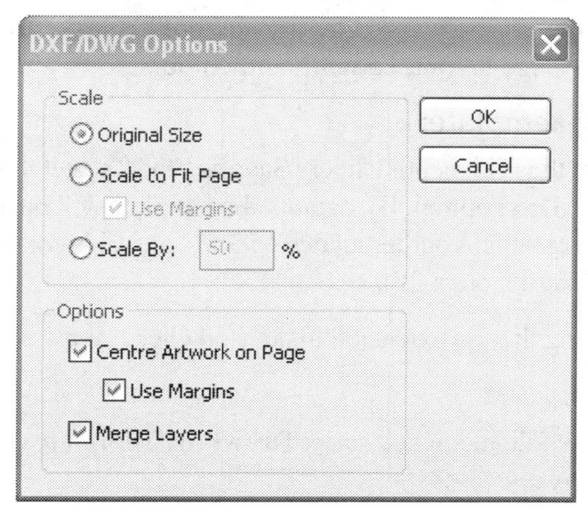

To open an AutoCad file:

1. Select **File>Open**.
2. Change the Files of type: drop-down menu to display **AutoCAD files (*.dwg,*.dxf)**, locate and select the name of the file, and click **Open**.
3. In the dialog (shown above), specify scaling and positioning options. Uncheck **Merge Layers** to retain the layer structure of the original AutoCad file—layers will automatically be shown in the Layers tab.
4. Click **OK**. The AutoCad drawing is opened.
5. Use **Save** or **Save As...** from the File menu to save as a DrawPlus Drawing (*.DPP).

Saving and Printing

- Click the **Save** button on the top toolbar and save your drawing.
- To print out your masterpiece, click the **Print** button (also on the top toolbar).

Using DrawPlus Templates

Templates help ensure continuity between drawings by preserving starting setups for such elements as page layout, content, and colours.

To save a drawing as a template:

1. Choose **Save As...** from the File menu. Under "Save as type:" select the **DrawPlus Template (*.Dpx)** option. By default, the template will be saved to a "My Templates" folder so that your templates will be accessible for future use (see Starting from Scratch on p. 28).
2. Enter a file name, leaving the file extension intact, and click **Save**.

To open a template file:

1. Choose **Open...** from the File menu and select **DrawPlus Template (*.Dpx)** in the "Files of type:" box.
2. Navigate to the folder containing your saved template file.
3. To open the original template, uncheck the **Open as untitled** option.
4. Click the **Open** button. You can then make edits to your template.

Viewing Pages

DrawPlus makes it easy to see exactly what you're working on—by using available **scrollbars**, **View toolbar** or the **Navigator tab**. For example, you can use the **scrollbars** at the right and bottom of the main window to move the page and pasteboard with respect to the main window. As you drag objects to the edge of the screen the scrollbars adjust automatically as the object is kept in view.

The **View toolbar** at the top of the screen hosts the **Pan Tool** as an alternative way of moving around, plus a number of buttons that let you **Zoom In** and **Zoom Out** so you can inspect and/or edit the page at different levels of detail.

If you're using a **wheel mouse**, you can scroll the wheel forward or back to move up or down the page, or move horizontally left or right by using the **Shift** key and scrolling together. Try combining the **Ctrl** key and scrolling up or down for immediate in/out zoom control.

The **Navigator tab** lets you quickly zoom into and pan around areas of your drawing.

Creating Borders

The **Border Wizard** lets you create a border around the whole page or a selected object, or within a specific page region.

To create a border:

1. (If creating a border around an object) Select the object first.
2. Click the **Border Wizard** button on the Insert menu.
3. Choose which type of border you want (whole page, around the current selection, or custom size and position) and click **Next**.
4. Choose one of the preset border styles from the scrolling list, and set the border's width. The preview window shows what the border will look like. Click **Finish**.

If you chose a whole-page or object border, it appears immediately. With the "custom" option, use the cursor to drag out a region to be bordered.

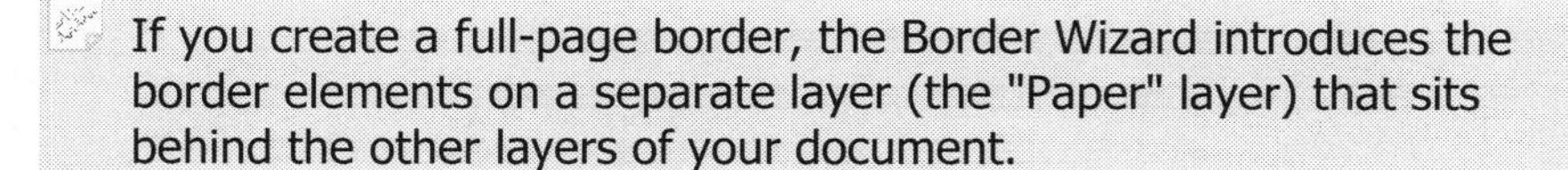
If you create a full-page border, the Border Wizard introduces the border elements on a separate layer (the "Paper" layer) that sits behind the other layers of your document.

Applying Paper Textures

Look no further than **paper textures** if you need to complement your drawing designs with a natural "paper-like" appearance. Simulate textures of varying roughness and "feel" by selection of various real media textures such as **Canvas**, **Cartridge**, **Embossed**, **Parchment**, and **Watercolour**. As a paper texture is applied to all objects on a specific layer you can apply different paper textures on a layer-by-layer basis.

To apply a paper texture:

1. In the Layers tab, select a layer on which objects are to be filled with a paper texture.
2. Click the **Apply Paper Texture** button and, from the dialog, select the **Paper Textures** category. A gallery of texture thumbnails is displayed.
3. Choose one of the thumbnails and adjust the percentage **Scale** and **Opacity** if needed.
4. Click **OK**. Existing or new objects will adopt the paper texture once applied.

To remove a paper texture:

1. Click on the layer which has paper textures applied to objects.
2. Click the **Apply Paper Texture** button.
3. From the dialog, select the **Remove** button. The paper texture is removed from all objects on the layer.

Using the Gallery

For an additional hand and to save you valuable design time, use the Gallery tab's pre-built designs to add to your drawings when appropriate. Gallery categories include Connecting Symbols (for electronics and family trees), Layout Symbols (for garden and home), SymbolArt, and ShapeArt (see Gel Shapes below). It's always worth checking the Gallery categories for possible artwork that can be incorporated into your drawing before striking out on your own! When you install the DrawPlus 8 Resource CD, the gallery tab will include further designs and design templates for your use.

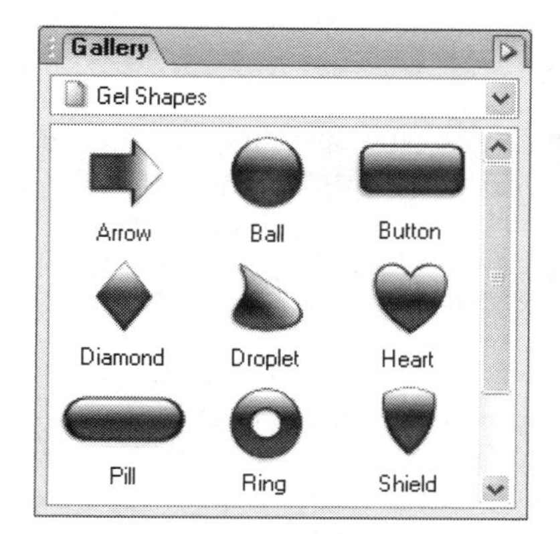

The Gallery tab also lets you store your own designs if you would like to reuse them—the design is made available in any DrawPlus document. You can add and delete your items within each category, with the option of naming elements to facilitate rapid retrieval.

You can even create your own design folders and categories under the **My Designs** section if you want to arrange a collection of your own designs.

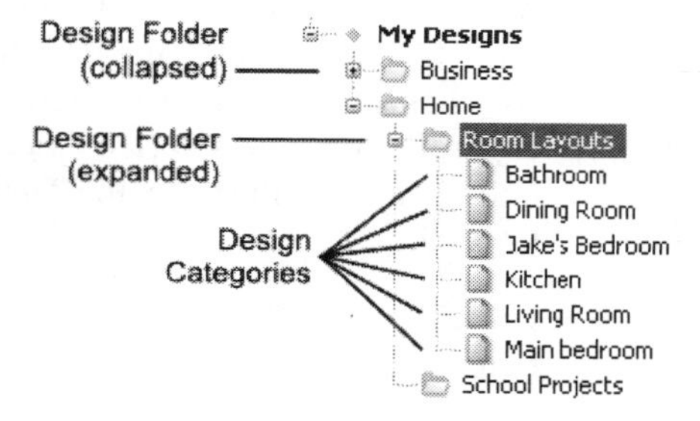

Closing DrawPlus

To close the current window:

- Choose **Close** from the File menu or click the window's × **Close** button. If it's the only window open, the command closes the window but leaves DrawPlus running. Either way you'll be prompted to save any unsaved changes.

To close DrawPlus:

- Choose **Exit** from the File menu.

You'll be prompted to save changes to any open documents.

Export Options

When you save a drawing, DrawPlus uses its own proprietary formats (.DPP for drawings, .DPX for templates and .DPA for animations) to store the information. From these formats it is possible to export your drawing as a graphic or simply print the drawing directly to a PDF file for electronic delivery/professional printing.

- **Export as graphics**: To be able to read the drawing into another application or use it on a Web page, the file needs to be saved in a suitable graphics format. You can do this at any time using the **File>Export...** command. This displays the powerful Export Optimizer, which lets you preview how your document will look in any available format. Before making up your mind, you can even compare side-by-side views using different export settings. You can use **File>Export...** to export one or more selected objects, too. For converting DrawPlus objects into pictures on the page, the **Tools>Convert to Bitmap...** command can be used.

- **Printing**: DrawPlus provides versatile printing capabilities to handle a range of document types, including multi-page documents; large-format posters and banners, folded documents such as cards or brochures, and various sheet and label formats. You can do both spot colour and process colour separations and set a wide range of prepress options for professional printing. And whether you're delivering work to a printer or sharing it over the Web, you can save a tree or two by exporting directly to the Adobe PDF format.

For full details on export options, see DrawPlus help (search on "exporting," "printing," or "PDF" in the Index) and Exporting your animation (p. 207) and Exporting graphics (p. 219).

Tutorial Resources

For more experience with the tools and techniques covered in this chapter, we recommend these PDF-based tutorials (go to **Help>Tutorials** in DrawPlus):

Try this tutorial...	For practice with these tools and techniques...
Create Filter Effects	Using the Startup Wizard
Explore the DrawPlus Gallery	Gallery tab, creating designs, ungrouping and editing SymbolArt

Jump between your PDF tutorials and DrawPlus with **Alt-Tab**.

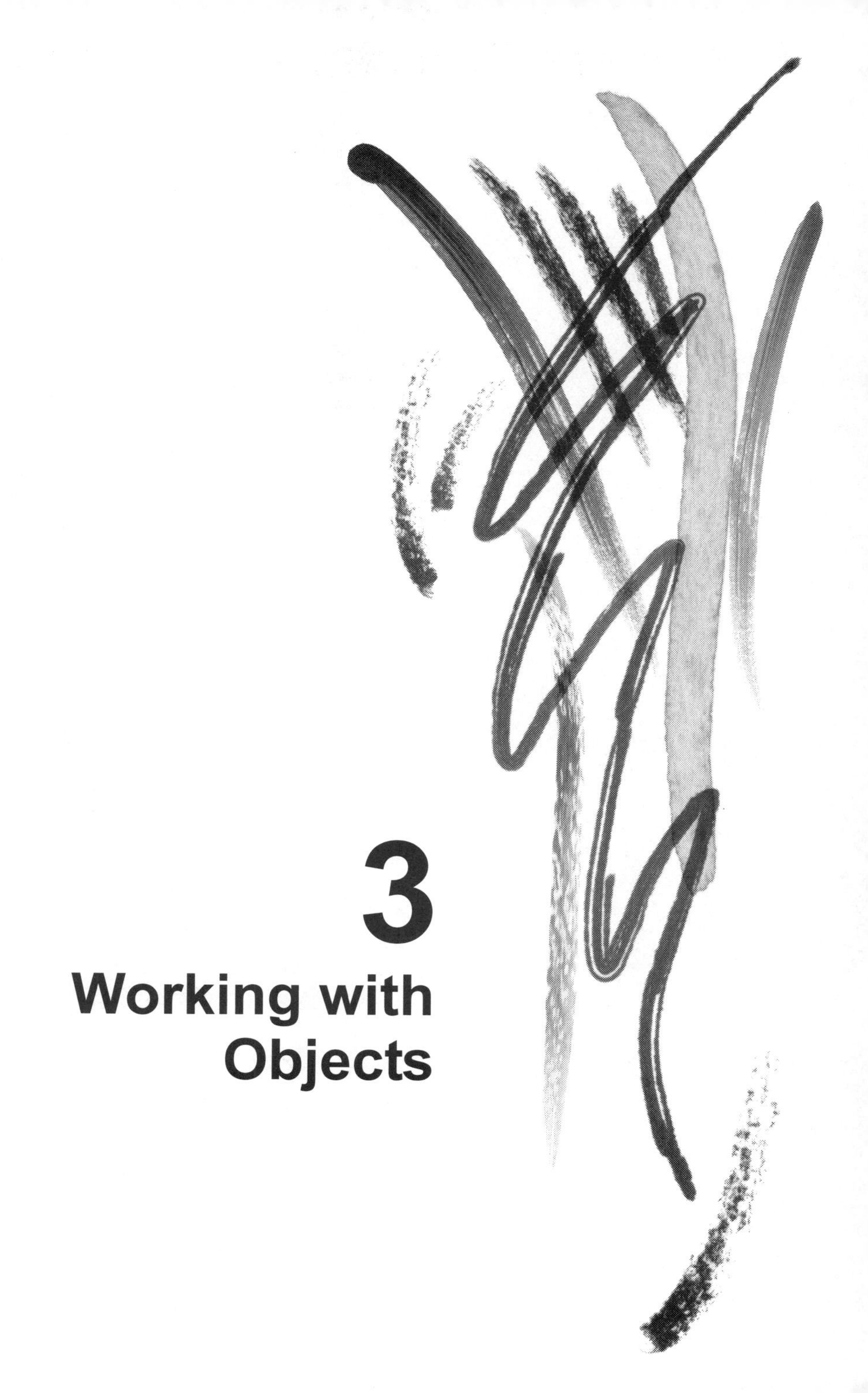

3
Working with Objects

Introduction

A DrawPlus drawing is made up of objects that can be picked up, moved and changed in many ways. If you were working with pencil and paper you would have to erase and redraw a shape to move it a little to the right. Using DrawPlus you can do the same job more directly and with far less work by picking the shape up and moving it to where you want it to be! If you want to think of a DrawPlus drawing in real-world terms, think of cut-out paper shapes with low-strength adhesive; not pencil and paper.

The Design Templates mentioned previously (p. 28) can be thought of as "object factories." They let you pick a design and leave you with one or more new objects on the page. If the design is exactly what you want then all that is left is for you to print it or export it. If you want to personalize the design or add to it then you need to know how to work with objects!

Types of Objects

DrawPlus can create three basic types of objects:

- Basic **lines** and shapes are created with the **Pencil**, **Pen** or **Straight Line** tools on the Drawing toolbar. The Pencil tool offers a freeform line, the Pen tool a curved line, while the Straight Line tool draws a straight line from A to B. They all consist of one or more **line segments** drawn between junction points called **nodes**. A **straight line** and a **curve** are basically lines with different kinds of nodes at each end. A **shape** is a line whose ends have been connected to form an enclosed region. We'll cover the fine points in Chapter 4, "Lines, Curves, and Shapes."

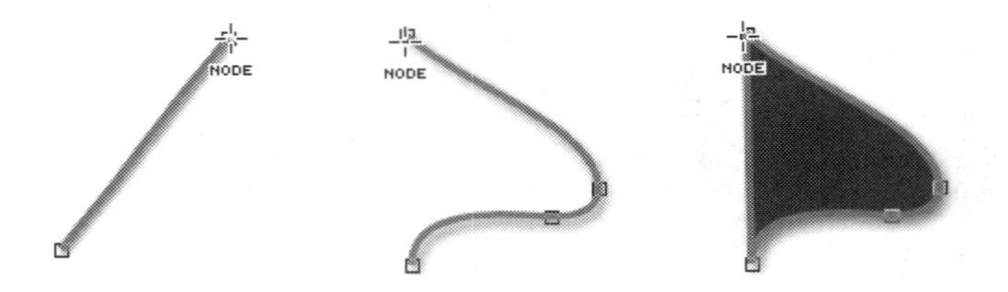

- **QuickShapes** are pre-designed objects that you can instantly add to your page, then adjust and vary using **control handles** (see centre Quick Star below). To create a QuickShape, you choose one from the **QuickShape flyout** on the Drawing toolbar, which contains a wide variety of commonly used shapes, including boxes, ovals, arrows, polygons and stars. See Chapter 6, "QuickShapes, Connectors, Text, and Pictures" for more details.

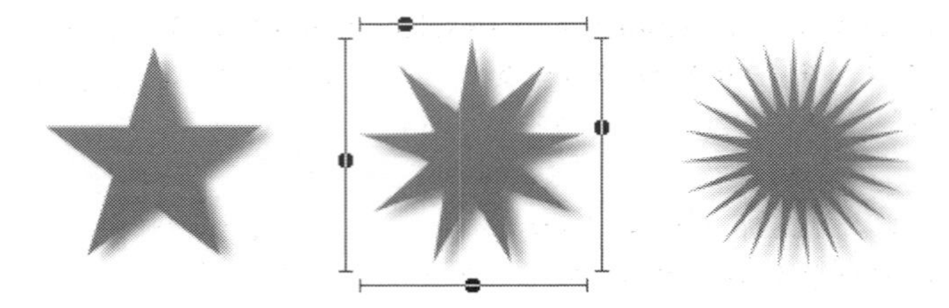

- **Text objects** are created with the **Text Tool**, either as standalone **free text** or as **shape text** typed into a containing shape. Either way, you can retype any text once it's created, and reformat the text in a variety of ways, e.g., align to a path or use a gradient fill. There's also a special dialog for editing text. Chapter 6, "QuickShapes, Connectors, Text, and Pictures" covers these in detail.

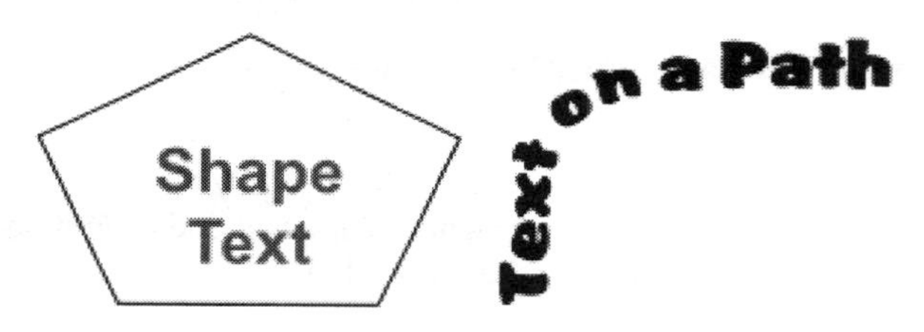

One thing that is common to all the above objects is that they can all be manipulated in a similar way, which we'll look at now.

Selecting

Before you can change any object, you need to select it using one of several tools from the Tools menu. At the top of the Drawing toolbar, above the creation tools, you'll find a group of three tools collectively known as the **selection tools**.

Pointer Tool
Click to use the **Pointer Tool** to select, move, copy, and resize objects.

Rotate Tool
Click to use the **Rotate Tool** to select then rotate objects to any angle or distort them by shearing. See Rotating or Shearing on p. 46 and 48, respectively.

Node Tool
Click to use the **Node Tool** to select then alter the shape of an object in very precise ways. See Editing Curves on p. 73.

To select an object:

- Click on the object using one of the tools shown above. For the Pointer and Rotate Tools, eight small "handles" appear around the object indicating selection. For the Node Tool, editable nodes are displayed for lines—sliding handles are shown for adjustment of QuickShapes and text.

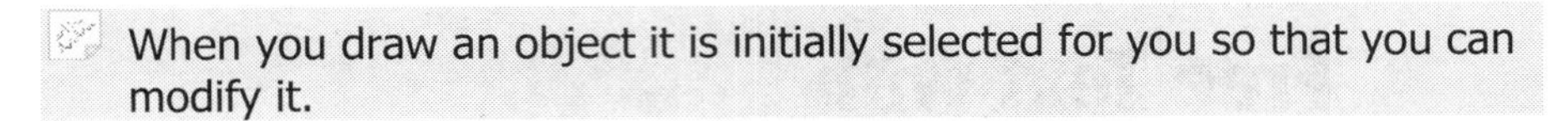

When you draw an object it is initially selected for you so that you can modify it.

To select objects as part of a group, see Grouping on p. 53.

Moving

You can move any selected object anywhere you want and drop it back onto the page or pasteboard by releasing the mouse button.

To move an object:

1. Select the **Pointer Tool**.
2. Click within the object and hold down your mouse button. Note that the Pointer cursor changed to become a Move cursor (a four-pointed arrow).

3. Drag the object to a new location then release the mouse button.

Alternatively, try pressing the keyboard arrow keys with an object selected. The object moves one step in the direction of each key press. If you hold down the **Ctrl** key at the same time, the object moves in 1/10 increments. Alternatively, set the **Nudge Distance** in **Tools >Options>Layout**.

For example, moving an object with the **Shift** key down restricts movement to the horizontal and vertical directions only.

For precise movements, you can enter exact X **Horizontal position** or Y **Vertical position** values in the **Transform** tab (see p. 167); then set an **Anchor point** to dictate from which part of the object the movement is to take place—from a corner, edge midpoint or centre.

Resizing

As well as moving a selected object you can also alter its size.

To resize an object:

1. Select an object. You'll see the object's eight handles appear.

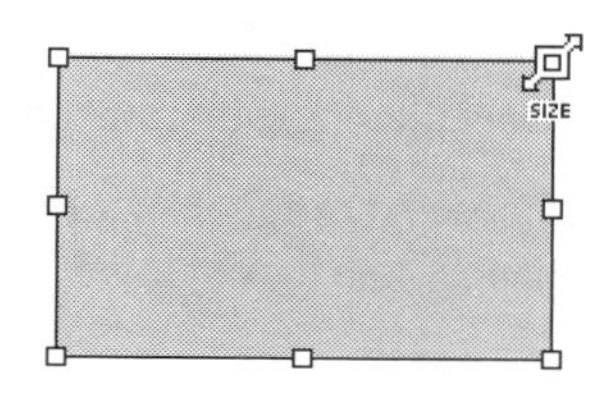

2. Choose the Pointer Tool **Pointer Tool** and position the pointer cursor over one of the object's handles—you will notice that the cursor changes to a double-headed Size cursor.
3. Hold the mouse button down and drag the handle—the object will grow or shrink accordingly. Simply dragging the corner handle produces a constrained (proportional) change in both the horizontal and vertical dimension—it maintains the aspect ratio.

To resize an object freely, hold down the **Shift** key while dragging a corner handle.

If you drag an object's side handles, you'll stretch or squash the object in one direction.

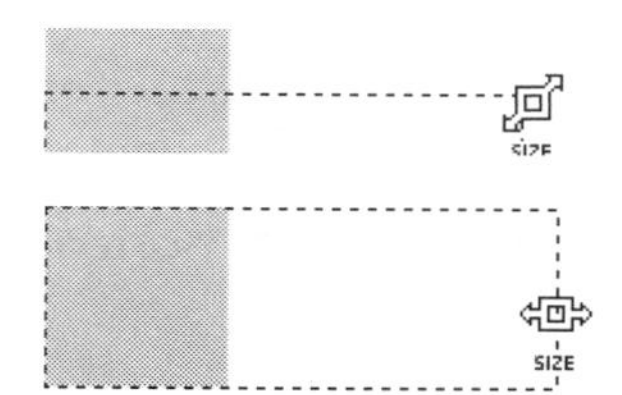

Another method of resizing is to use the keyboard arrows while pressing the **Shift** key. The object's upper left corner remains fixed, while its right and bottom edges move according to the arrow key pressed. For extra-fine size adjustments, press both the **Shift** and **Ctrl** keys at the same time.

Use **Arrange>Size items** to simultaneously resize objects to an object selected last in a Shift-click group selection.

For precise resizing, you may wish to use Rulers and Guides along with Snapping while manipulating your objects (see p. 163). Additionally, you can enter exact H **Height** and W **Width** values in the **Transform** tab (see p. 167); then set an **Anchor point** to dictate which part of the object the resizing is to take place—from a corner, edge midpoint or centre.

Locking an Object's Position

So you may have moved or resized a few objects and don't want to risk moving, resizing or deleting them. The solution is to lock them to prevent accidental changes from occurring.

To lock an object:

1. Select the single or grouped object.
2. Choose **Arrange>Lock Position**. When you try to select the object the cursor changes to a lock symbol.

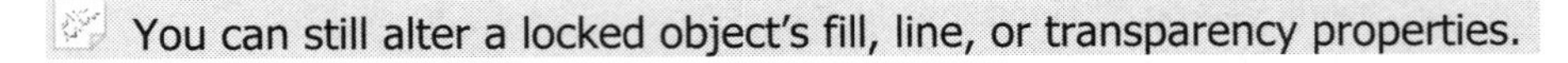

You can still alter a locked object's fill, line, or transparency properties.

To unlock an object:

1. Select the single or grouped object.
2. Use the **Arrange>Unlock Position** command. Now you'll see a normal cursor and selection handles again.

Flipping

You can flip objects horizontally (left to right; top and bottom stay the same) or vertically (top to bottom; left and right stay the same).

To flip an object horizontally/vertically:

1. Select the object.
2. Choose **Flip Horizontal** or **Flip Vertical** on the Standard toolbar.

Rotating

To rotate a selected object you use the Rotate Tool (you can also select objects with the tool). The difference is that the selected objects are displayed with a different set of handles appropriate for the tool.

To rotate an object:

1. Select the Rotate Tool on the Drawing toolbar.
2. Click to select the object, hover over one of its handles until you see the rotate pointer (below).

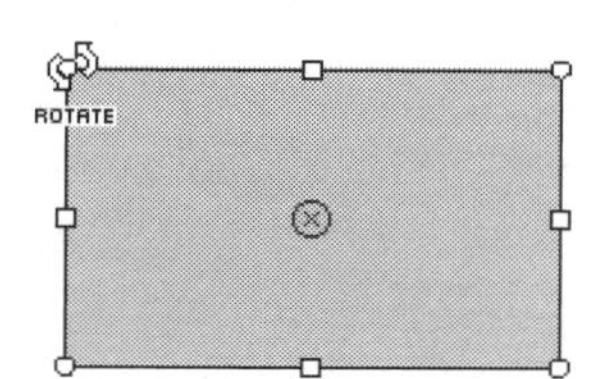

3. Hold the mouse down and drag the pointer in the direction in which you want to rotate the object, then release (use **Shift** key for 15 degree intervals). The object is rotated about its centre of rotation ⊗.

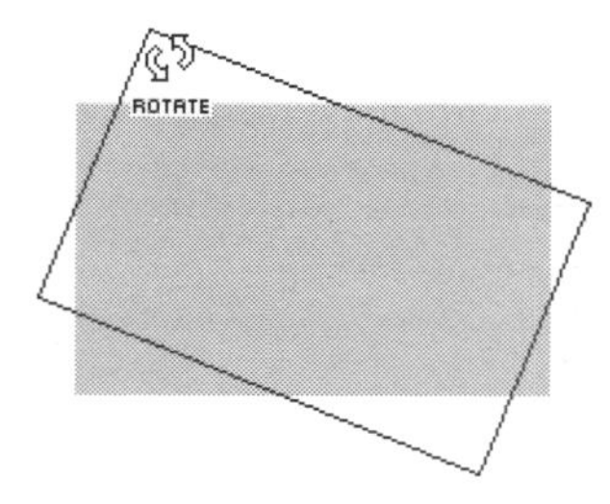

Any rotation can be undone by double-clicking on the object.

For anticlockwise rotation at 90° intervals consider using the **Rotate 90°** button on the Standard toolbar.

To change the centre of rotation:

1. Move the centre of rotation ⊗ away from its original position to any position on the page.
2. Drag the rotate pointer to a new rotation angle—the object will rotate about the new pivot.

For precise rotations, enter an exact **Object rotation** value in the **Transform** tab (see p. 167); then set an **Anchor point** to dictate which part of the object the rotation is to take place—from a corner, edge midpoint or centre.

Shearing

Besides being able to rotate an object, the Rotate Tool allows you to skew or "shear" it.

To shear an object:

1. Select the **Rotate Tool** on the Drawing toolbar.
2. Click to select the object, hover over any side handle (not a corner handle) until you see the Shear cursor.

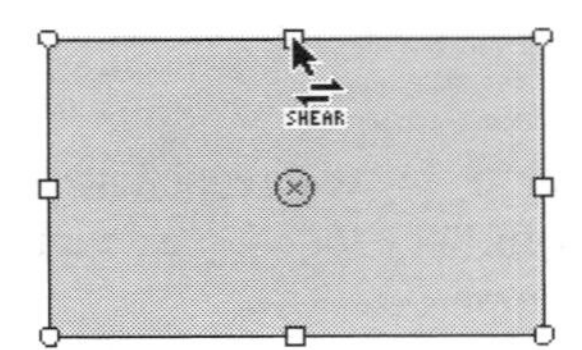

3. Hold the mouse down and drag the pointer in the direction in which you want to shear the object, then release.

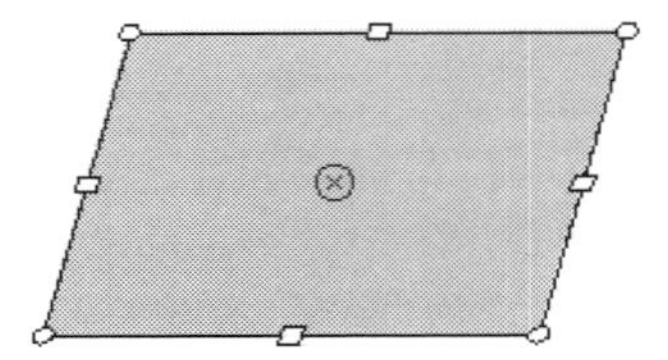

For precise shearing operations, you can enter an exact **Shear** value in the **Transform** tab (see p. 167); then set an **Anchor point** to dictate which part of the object the shearing is to take place—from a corner, edge midpoint or centre.

Any shearing operation can be undone by double-clicking on the object.

Alternatively, for more sophisticated dimensional skew effects, try applying one of the presets on the Perspective Tool's context toolbar. For details, see p. 191.

Deleting

To delete an object:

- Select the object with the Pointer Tool and press the **Delete** key. (You can also choose **Clear** from the Edit menu.)

Changing your Mind

After mentioning deletion, it's worth introducing a quick and easy way of undoing your mistakes! You can reverse any operation on a drawing at any time.

To undo an action:

- Click the **Undo** button on the Standard toolbar.
  OR
  Press **Ctrl+Z**.
  OR
  Choose the **Edit>Undo** menu command.

The command as shown in the menu will actually name the action that it will undo. For example, if you have just deleted an object using the **Edit>Clear** command the Undo menu item will become **Undo Clear**. In this way you can always be sure what you are "undoing"!

To redo an action:

- Click the **Redo** button on the Standard toolbar.
  OR
  Press **Ctrl+Y**.
  OR
  Choose the **Edit>Redo** menu command.

To undo or redo multiple changes with a single action, click the down arrow of the Undo or Redo button, drag down to highlight the number of actions you wish to undo/redo to, then release the mouse button. You can change the number of stored undo/redo actions in the General pane of the **Tools>Options...** dialog. This can be used as a repeat function for some actions (e.g., move).

Cut, Copy, Paste and Duplicate

Besides using the Windows Clipboard to cut, copy and paste objects, you can duplicate objects easily using drag-and-drop, and duplicate multiple copies of any object. For duplication, a copy is displayed at the new location and the original object is still kept at the same position—your new copy also possesses the formatting of the original copied object.

To cut an object to the Windows Clipboard:

1. Select the object.
2. Click the **Cut** button on the Standard toolbar.
   OR
   Select **Edit>Cut**.
   OR
   Type **Ctrl+X**.

To copy an object to the Windows Clipboard:

1. Select the object(s).
2. Click the **Copy** button on the Standard toolbar.
   OR
   Select **Edit>Copy**.
   OR
   Type **Ctrl+C**.

If you're using another Windows application, you can usually copy and paste objects via the Clipboard.

To paste an object from the Clipboard:

- Click the **Paste** button on the Standard toolbar.
  OR
  Select **Edit>Paste**.
  OR
  Type **Ctrl+V**.

The standard Paste command inserts a clipboard object onto the page.

To choose between alternative Clipboard formats:

- Choose **Paste Special...** from the Edit menu.

To duplicate an object:

1. Select the object, then press the **Ctrl** key. The cursor changes to the Copy cursor.

2. Drag the object to a new location on the page, keeping the **Ctrl** key pressed throughout.

To constrain the position of the copy (to same horizontal or vertical), press and hold down the **Shift** key simultaneously while dragging. A duplicate of the object appears at the new location.

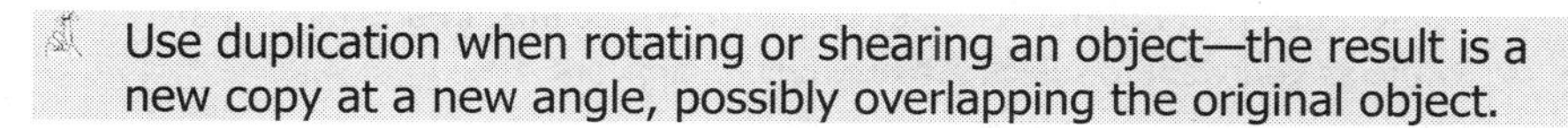
Use duplication when rotating or shearing an object—the result is a new copy at a new angle, possibly overlapping the original object.

Replicating

If you need to clone single or multiple objects, you can use the Replicate feature to avoid repetitive copy and paste operations. For example, you can specify three columns and four rows, for twelve identical copies. The tool comes in handy for creating repetitive patterns or producing artwork for label sheets.

To replicate an object:

1. Select an object. Remember to size the object to be cloned and place it in a convenient starting position—usually the top-left of the page.
2. Choose **Replicate...** from the Tools menu.
3. In the dialog, set the Grid size by choosing number of columns or rows. Objects are cloned into this grid arrangement (but can be moved subsequently into any position).
4. Set an X and Y spacing (horizontal and vertical gap) between objects if necessary.
5. Click **OK**.

Notes

For multiple objects on different layers, you can right-click on a layer and check the item **Edit All Layers**. Now, instead of working with the layers one at a time, we can include all objects (once selected) on all layers, permitting perfect replication.

Selecting Multiple Objects

Up to now we have been concerned with selecting and manipulating a single object. However, it is possible to select more than one object at one time. A set of objects selected in this way forms a **multiple selection** that you can manipulate as if it were one object, or turn into a group object. For now, the question is how to select more than one object at a time? There are two methods to choose from.

To select multiple objects with Pointer Tool:

1. Draw several objects on your drawing. These could be Quickshapes, lines, text, etc.
2. Select the **Pointer Tool** to drag a **marquee box** around those drawn objects you want to select. An outline box appears.

3. Release the mouse button. All of the objects within the marquee box are selected and one selection box, with handles, appears around the objects.

To select multiple objects with Shift key:

1. Click on the first object for selection.
2. Press the **Shift** key down then click on a second object. Notice how the selection handles now encompass both objects.
3. Continue selecting other objects to build up your multiple selection.

The multiple selection can be sized, rotated, skewed, copied, deleted, and so on, in one operation as if it were a single object.

Once you click away from the multiple selection they are deselected and become individual objects again! If you require your objects to stay together more permanently you can always group the objects together (see p. 53).

Use **Shift**-click to add/remove an object to an existing multiple selection.

Selecting multiple objects by either of the above methods produces very different results when objects are aligned (see p. 58).

Selecting Overlapping Objects

When you have multiple selections where objects overlap the job of selecting a specific one becomes a little more complex. How do you select an object that is “behind” other objects?

To select an overlapped object:

- Click on a portion of the overlapped object if visible.
  OR
- Repeatedly click with the mouse over the objects. Each time you click at the same location, a different object in the stack is selected, allowing you to select any of the overlapping objects.
  OR
- Press **Tab** repeatedly to cycle through every object in the drawing, so that you can even get to objects you can't see. Pressing **Tab+Shift** cycles in the opposite direction.

Grouping

The advantage of converting a set of objects into a group is that it is easier to select and edit the objects all at the same time. The only requirement for grouping is that multiple objects are selected in advance (see p. 52).

Simply clicking on any member of a group selects the group object. In general, any operation you carry out on a selected group affects each member of the group.

Objects within groups can be selected and edited without having to ungroup your grouped objects. Text can be edited, the Node Tool applied, line and fill properties can be changed. In fact you can edit any grouped object as you would its ungrouped counterpart. This avoids the headache of having to reassemble the group after editing an individual object!

To create a group from a multiple selection:

1. Select multiple objects.
2. Click the **Group/Ungroup** button on the Standard toolbar. The HintLine tells you when a group is selected, or you can check the state of the **Group/Ungroup** button (up or down).

To ungroup:

1. Select the object group.
2. Click the **Group/Ungroup** button on the Standard toolbar to turn back to a multiple selection.

To select an object in a group:

1. Select the object group.
2. Press the **Ctrl** key while selecting the individual object which requires editing. The object is selected as for any ungrouped object.
3. Perform your edit on the object then click away to deselect the group.

You can additionally use the **Shift** key to select and edit multiple objects within the group.

Ordering

If the concept of ordering is new to you, think of the objects on a page as being stacked or piled on top of each other. The frontmost object is the one on top of the stack. Each time you create a new object, it goes in front of the objects already there. But you can move any object to any level in the ordering sequence, and obtain sophisticated drawing effects by learning how to manipulate the front/back relationship of objects.

There are four possibilities for ordering objects but not all of them are always available. If you have selected an object that is on top of all others you will have the options **Send to Back** and **Back One** - you can't bring it forward because it's on the top "level" of the stack. Conversely, for an object at the bottom of a stack you will have the options **Bring to Front** or **Forward One**. All the options are available for objects that are neither at the top or bottom.

To change the object's position in the stacking order:

- To shift the selected object's position behind other objects, choose the **Send to Back** button from the Standard toolbar or **Arrange>Order Objects>Send to Back**.
- To shift the selected object's position to the front of other objects, choose the **Bring to Front** button from the Standard toolbar or **Arrange>Order Objects>Bring to Front**.
- To shift the object's position one step toward the front, choose **Arrange>Order Objects>Forward One**.
- To shift the object's position one step toward the back, and choose **Arrange>Order Objects>Back One**.

Combining

DrawPlus includes some powerful tools to carve new shapes out of old shapes—the **Combine**, **Crop**, **Clip**, **Add**, **Subtract**, and **Intersect** buttons on the Standard toolbar! Combine, Crop and Clip work a bit differently from Add, Subtract and Intersect (considered as "Join" commands). It's worth keeping the distinctions in mind:

- With Combine, Crop and Clip, you're creating a temporary composite object where two or more component objects used to overlap. This combination, like a group, can be broken apart later with **Crop>Uncrop** on the Arrange menu.
- With the Join commands, you actually produce a permanent new object out of any selected objects. The action can't be reversed, except by using the Undo command. A Joined object can be edited with the Node Tool, while a combined, cropped or clipped object cannot.

Now let's see how the commands actually work. In all cases, you first have to select the objects you want to combine, crop, clip or join, then click the appropriate button.

We'll use the same two overlapping objects to perform each operation on, i.e.

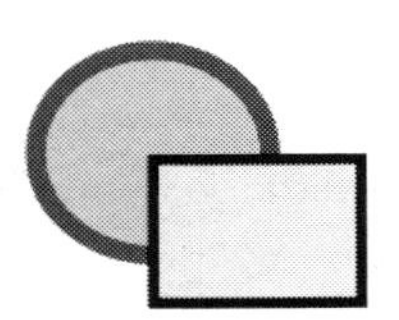

Icon	Name	Description	Example
	Combine	Merges two or more objects into a composite object, with a clear "hole" where their filled regions overlap. The composite takes the line and fill of the bottom object. Click button again to **Break Apart**.	
	Crop and Clip flyout	Provides four cropping or clipping functions as follows:	
	• Crop to Top	The bottom object is cropped to the outline of the top object.	
	• Crop to Bottom	The top object is cropped to the outline of the bottom object.	
	• Clip to Top	The bottom object is clipped to the outline of the top object.	

	• Clip to Bottom	The top object is clipped to the outline of the bottom object.	
	**Join/Add**	Creates one new object that's the sum of any selected objects, whether or not they overlap.	
	**Join/Subtract**	Discards the overlap between the top and bottom object. The top object is also discarded.	
	**Join/Intersect**	like Subtract, requires overlapping objects—it retains the overlap and discards the rest.	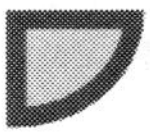

If only one object, rather than a multiple selection, is selected, Combine automatically gives a mask or stencil effect by combining the selected object with a rectangle. The object becomes a transparent window inside the rectangle

Aligning and Distributing

Alignment involves taking a group of selected objects and aligning them all in one operation—the operation is applied to all of the objects selected. The alignment's behaviour is different depending on how multiple objects are selected, i.e.

- **by Shift-click**: If you select each object in turn by **Shift**-click, the alignment of selected objects is always performed relative to the edges of the last selected object (unless alignment relative to the page is set).
- **by Marquee**: If you drag a marquee over the objects (or use **Edit>Select All**), the objects are always aligned relative to the edges of the object which is farthest back in the z-order (unless alignment relative to the page is set).

For example, top alignment will align objects to the top edge of the square (shown below) if it was selected last or if all objects were selected by marquee (assumes the square is the farthest back object). Bottom alignment would align to the bottom edge of the square.

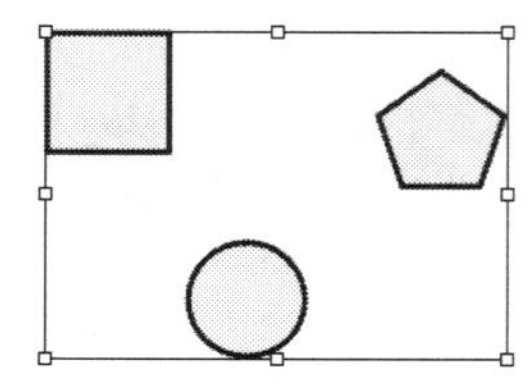

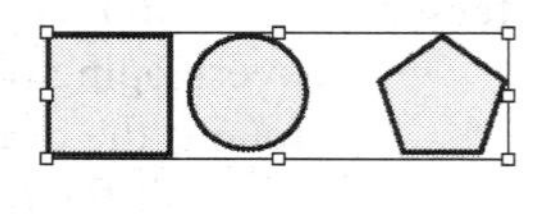

Alignment controls are available in the **Align** tab or from **Arrange>Align Objects**. Both sets of controls let you **distribute** objects, so that your objects are spread evenly across your page. Use **Space Evenly** to keep the endmost items in the same position. Or, for a specific distance between each object, select the **Vertical Distribute** or **Horizontal Distribute** option, then type the size of gap to be inserted between the objects.

Align Top
Aligns to object[1] top edge or the top of the page.

Align Bottom
Aligns to object[1] bottom edge or the bottom of the page.

Align Left
Aligns to object[1] left edge or the left of the page.

Align Right
Aligns to object[1] right edge or the right of the page.

Horizontal Centre
Horizontally aligns to object[1] centre or the page centre.

Vertical Centre
Vertically aligns to object[1] centre or the page centre.

Spaced
Check to enable spacing of distributed objects horizontally or vertically. If checked, use the adjacent input box to set a distance by which objects are to be spaced. If unchecked, objects are spread evenly between the two endmost items. Applies to **Horizontal Distribute** and **Vertical Distribute** options only.

Horizontal Distribute
Spreads the selected objects horizontally—either evenly between the endmost items or by a set amount of spacing (see Spaced).

Vertical Distribute
Spreads the selected objects vertically—either evenly between the endmost items or by a set amount of spacing (see Spaced).

Include Page
If selected the page is added to the set of objects included in the alignment, e.g. selecting **Top** aligns all of the objects in the selection to the top of the page.

[1]Object is the last selected object for **Shift**-click multiple selection or the farthest back in z-order for **marquee** multiple selection.

To align two or more objects:

1. Using the **Pointer Tool**, Shift-click on all the objects you want to align, or draw a marquee box around them (or use **Edit>Select All**), to create a multiple selection.
2. In the Align tab, select an option for vertical (Top, Vertical Centre, or Bottom) and/or horizontal (Left, Horizontal Centre, Right) alignment.
3. Check the **Include Page** option to include the page in the alignment.

Remember that the alignment behaviour is dependent on selection method.

To distribute two or more objects:

1. Using the **Pointer Tool**, Shift-click on all the objects you want to distribute, or draw a marquee box around them, to create a multiple selection.
2. In the Align tab, select the **Vertical Distribute** or **Horizontal Distribute** option to distribute objects vertically or horizontally, respectively.
3. Check the **Spaced** option to set a fixed distance between vertically or horizontally distributed objects (otherwise the objects distribute evenly between endmost items).

Using Object Defaults

When you create new objects in DrawPlus, the way they look depends on the current default settings for that particular type of object. DrawPlus stores defaults separately for (1) **lines/shapes** (including **QuickShapes**), (2) **free text objects**, (3) **connectors**, (4) **dimension objects** and (5) **brushes**. Defaults for shape text (as contained in shapes) are distinct from those for free text, and are defined along with other shape defaults. Default properties for lines and shapes include **line** and **fill**. Initially, the default line is black with a weight of 1.0 pixel, and the default fill is "None."

You can use several methods to change the default object settings according to your preferred way or working. Each technique differs depending on the current **Synchronize Defaults** setting on the Standard toolbar, i.e.

- Defaults are changed by **manually** updating to the current object selection, and apply until they are manually updated again. Only use when **Synchronize Defaults** is disabled (unchecked).
- Defaults are changed **dynamically** by adopting the attributes of the currently selected object. This is possible when **Synchronize Defaults** is enabled (checked).

To see what the current defaults are for a particular object type, simply create a new object of that type.

To set object defaults manually:

1. Create a sample object (the object type matching the set of defaults you're updating: line/shape, free text object, connector, or dimension object), and alter it to use the specific properties you plan to use as defaults.
2. Right-click the object and choose **Update Defaults** (or choose **Update Object Defaults** from the Format menu).

When you update defaults from a shape, all default shape properties, including **shape text** attributes, are reset at the same time. To avoid altering these settings when updating only shape text defaults, create a new sample shape and modify only its text.

Normally, each time you close a document, object default settings are recorded as "master settings" to be used in future documents. To change whether DrawPlus records the defaults as master settings, choose **Tools>Save Settings...** and check/uncheck the **Object Defaults** box.

To set object defaults dynamically:

1. If disabled, check **Synchronize Defaults** on the flyout on the Standard toolbar (enabled by default).
2. Choose **Synchronize Settings...** from the same flyout to optionally select attributes (e.g., Fill colour, Line colour, Transparency, etc) from which new defaults will be made.
3. Begin drawing to establish some objects on the page—continue changing object attributes via the context bars or tabs. Note that subsequently drawn objects adopt the attributes of the last selected object.

More about Synchronizing Defaults

The **Synchronize Defaults** feature is particularly useful when you want to quickly inherit the attributes of a currently selected object, e.g. when painting, you might want to reuse the colour of a previously painted brush stroke.

Choosing object attributes

When you select the **Synchronize Settings**, a pop-up dialog lets you check on or off selected attributes which synchronize with, or update to, the currently selected object.

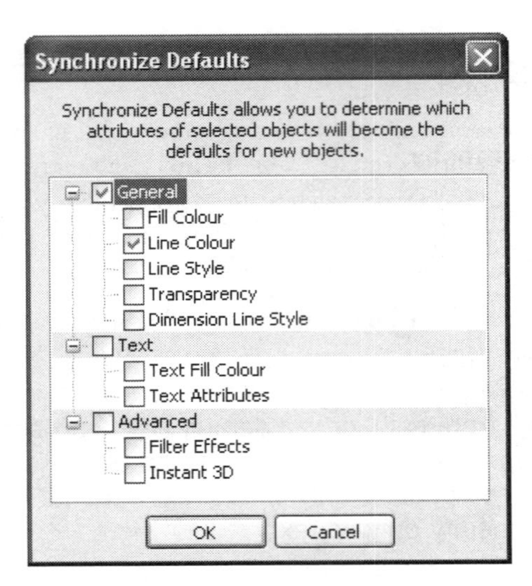

In the above example, only the last selected object's line colour is used for future drawing. If you subsequently change a line colour's attributes, then the defaults will be updated automatically.

Resetting Defaults

Two methods for resetting defaults exist—one for a global reset of object defaults and one for resetting only the currently selected object's defaults.

The former method is useful if you feel the need to get back to basics and reset to DrawPlus's original default settings—a simple click of **Reset Defaults** from the **Synchronize Defaults** flyout (Standard toolbar) is all that is needed. This also affects any currently selected objects.

The latter method can be used to "revert" selected object attributes back to application defaults. This means that you can localize format control, i.e. the global defaults are not affected. Select the **Reset Current Object Defaults** option from the Standard toolbar directly.

Tutorial Resources

For more experience with the tools and techniques covered in this chapter, we recommend these PDF-based tutorials (go to **Help>Tutorials** in DrawPlus):

Try this tutorial...	For practice with these tools and techniques...
Create a Velvet Effect	Aligning Objects
Create an 8-Ball	Flipping Objects
Create Shadows and Clouds	Rotating Objects
Create a Warped Film Strip	Replicating Objects
Create Filter Effects	Combine Tool

Jump between your PDF tutorials and DrawPlus with **Alt-Tab**.

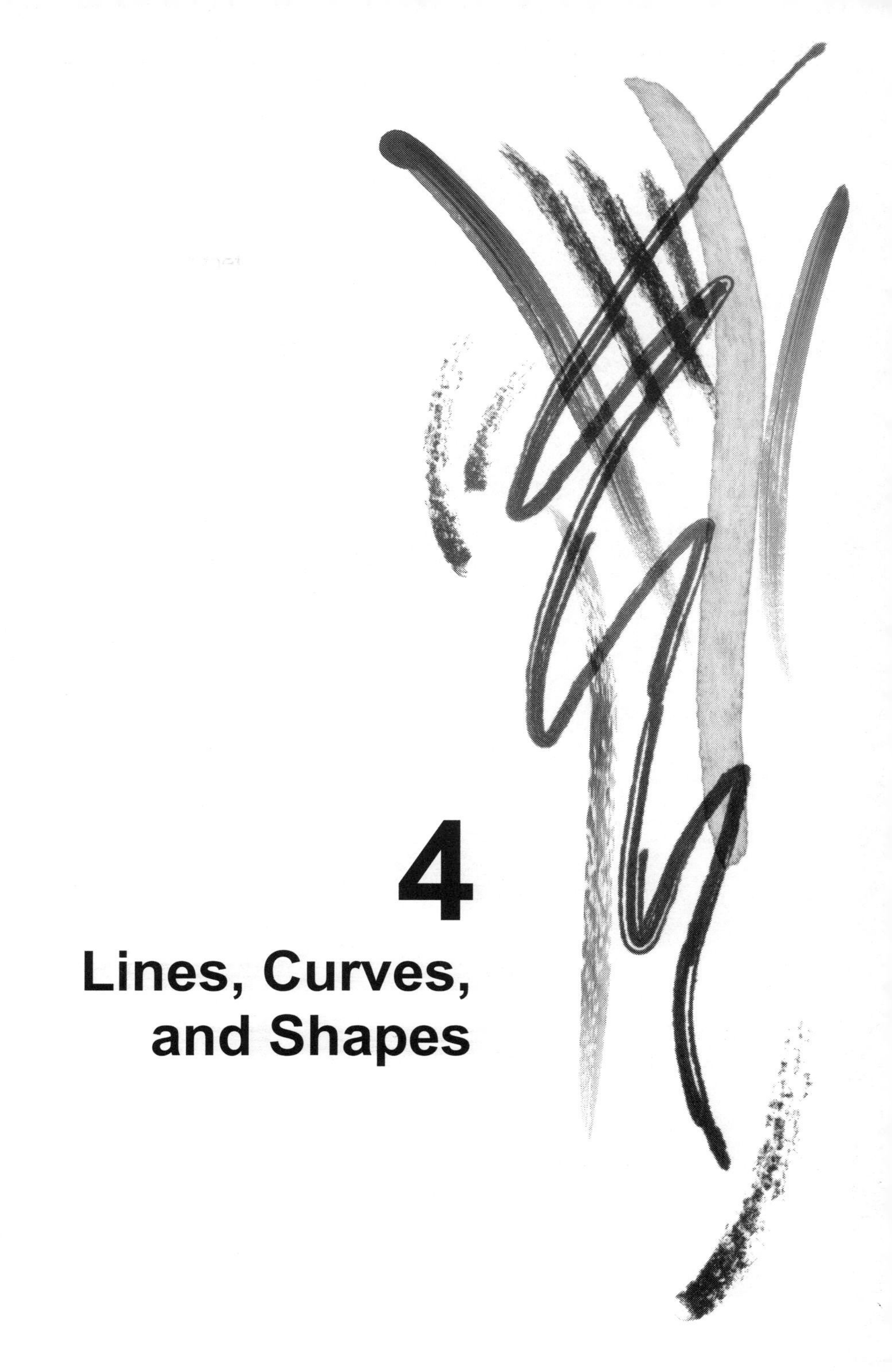

4
Lines, Curves, and Shapes

Introduction

Lines, curves, and shapes are all variations of one basic object: the line. They all consist of one or more **line segments** drawn between junction points called **nodes**. In general, if we use the word "line" it can mean either a **straight line** or a **curve**. A **shape** is a line whose ends have been connected to form an enclosed region.

Line art offers an unlimited opportunity to draw not only the basic line, but many other curves and object borders which are considered line based. A vast array of effects and tools can be applied such that you are limited only by your imagination. Consider a few interesting types of line art ...all possible from within DrawPlus.

Properties of lines and shapes

Lines can be either straight or curved. They have **line properties** like colour and weight (thickness). When you draw a new line, it takes on the current **default** line properties (see p. 60).

Because shapes have an interior region that can be filled (for example, with a solid colour or a bitmap), they have **fill properties** as well as line properties. The interior region takes on the default fill as soon as a line is closed to become a shape; initially the default setting is for no fill.

Lets' look firstly at drawing basic lines and shapes and then explore how to modify lines and shapes, achieving precise control over the results.

Drawing Basic Lines, Curves and Shapes

DrawPlus provides the **Pencil**, **Pen**, and **Straight Line** tools for creating simple line graphics. Using these tools, you can draw single lines and connect line segments together.

The **Pencil Tool** lets you sketch curved lines and shapes in a freeform way.

The **Pen Tool** lets you join a series of line segments (which may be curved or straight) using "connect the dots" mouse clicks. New line segments are added all the time. The tool is designed for drawing complex, combination curves and shapes in a highly controlled way.

The **Straight Line Tool** is used exclusively for drawing straight lines.

Drawing Lines

To draw a freeform line (with the Pencil Tool):

1. Choose the **Pencil Tool** from the Drawing toolbar. Immediately, you'll notice a **Pencil context toolbar** display above your workspace.
2. Click once, then drag across the page, drawing a line as you go.
3. To end the line, release the mouse button. The line will automatically smooth out using a minimal number of nodes. Note the dots indicating its nodes—at the two ends, and at each point where two line segments come together.

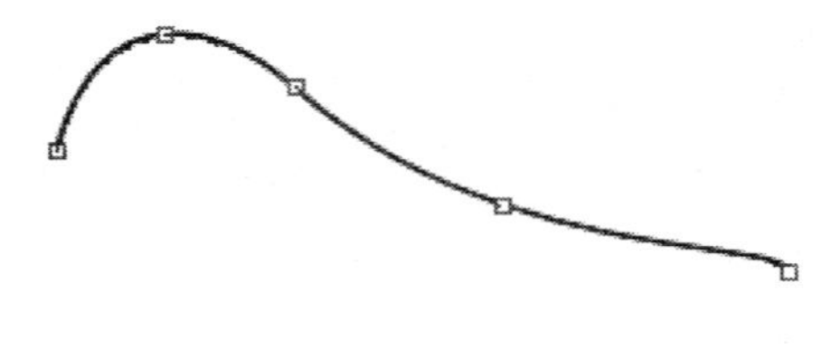

4. On the Pencil context toolbar, you'll see the **Smoothness** setting.

Click its right arrow to display a slider—drag right, then left. You'll see your drawn line—still selected—smooth out (with fewer nodes) as you drag right, and become more jagged (with more nodes) as you drag left. This option can work wonders to improve your confidence when drawing onscreen, something few of us are good at. For the smoothest curves the next time you draw a freeform line, leave the sliding arrow towards the left of the slider.

Using a pen tablet but not too sure of your freehand drawing ability? As a solution, select the Pencil Tool, then with the tablet pen either:

- Draw freehand or accurate lines with a ruler on the tablet.
  OR
- Place any printed image on your tablet and just trace around its outlines.

Still not drawing accurately? Then switch to the **Node Tool** and fine-tune the line to be closer to what you envisaged.

To draw one or more line segments (with the Pen Tool):

1. Choose the **Pen Tool** from the Drawing toolbar. The **Pen context toolbar** appears, which hosts buttons that let you select the segment you'll draw.

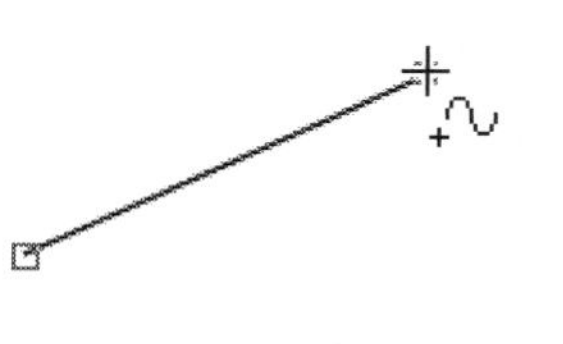

A **Straight** segment is simply a straight line connecting two nodes. (Shortcut: Press **1**)

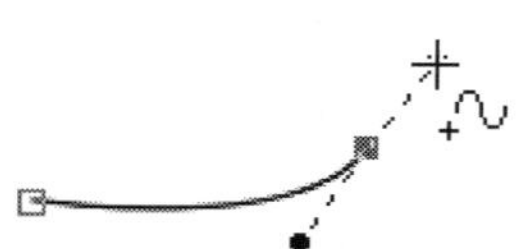

A **Custom** (Bézier) segment is curved, displaying control handles for precise adjustment. (Shortcut: Press **2**)

Smart segments (default) appear without visible control handles, using automatic curve-fitting to connect each node. (Shortcut: Press **3**)

2. Select a segment type, then click where you want the line to start.

- For a **Straight** segment, just click again (or drag) for a new node where you want the segment to end.
- For a **Custom** segment, click again for a new node and drag out a pair of **control handles** which orbit the node. (Control handles act like "magnets," pulling the curve into shape. The distance between handles determines the depth of the resulting curved line.) Click again where you want the segment to end, and a curved segment appears.
- For a **Smart** segment, click again for a new node. The segment appears as a smooth, best-fitting curve (without visible control handles) between the new node and the preceding node. Before releasing the mouse button, you can drag to "flex" the line as if bending a piece of wire. If the preceding corner node on the line is also smart, flexibility extends back to the preceding segment.

3. To end the line, press **Esc** or choose a different tool.

To select the opposite end node of the curve (i.e., to extend the curve from the other end), press **Tab** before drawing the next segment.

Use **Shift**-click to align a Straight, Custom or Smart segment at 90 degree intervals (useful for quick right-angle junctions) with respect to the node.

You can reshape the line after it's drawn (see below) or apply different weight, colour, or other attributes (see Applying line properties on p. 143).

To draw a straight line (with the Straight Line Tool):

1. Click the Line button on the Drawing toolbar and choose the **Straight Line Tool** from the flyout. The flyout icon will always reflect the last tool selected.
2. Click where you want the line to start, and drag to another point while holding down the mouse button, then release the mouse button. The line appears immediately.

Extending lines

Any kind of **open line** (that is, one that hasn't been closed to create a shape) can be extended, and you can use any of the three line tools to do so. Use the Pointer Tool and then the line's drawing tool to resize or reshape lines once you've drawn them.

For example, suppose you've drawn a freeform line with the **Pencil Tool**. When you release the mouse button the curve you've drawn is displayed with two red nodes at each end.

Now if you move the cursor over either of the nodes, a small + sign will appear. Click at that location, and the next line that you drag out will be a continuation of the existing line.

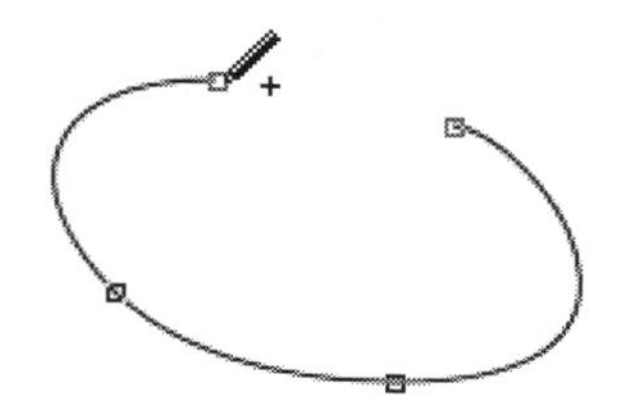

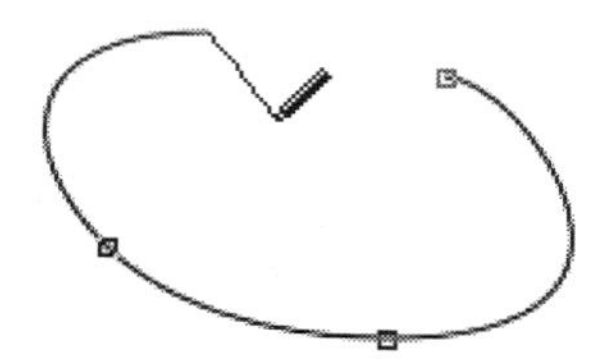

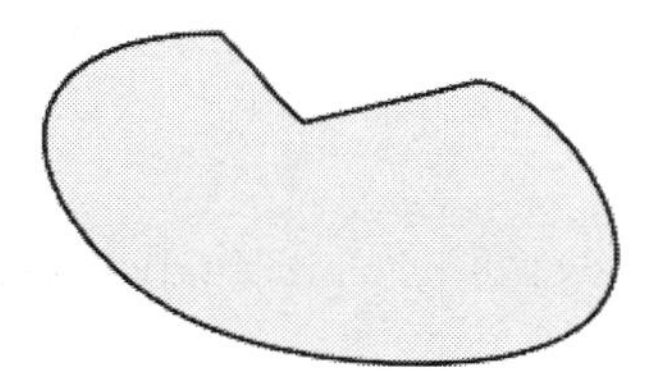

Remember, you can use this technique with any kind of line and with any of the line tools to build up a long line—drawing a line between one end node and the other, you can close the curve, creating a new shape that can take a fill!

Redrawing Lines

The Pencil or Straight Line tools let you redraw any section of a line.

To redraw a line:

1. Select the line, then the **Pencil Tool** or **Straight Line Tool**. Hover the displayed cursor on the line where you want to begin redrawing. The cursor changes to indicate you can begin redrawing.

2. Pick a starting point somewhere along the line, then click and a new node appears immediately.

3. Keep the mouse button down and drag to draw a new line section, connecting it back to another point on the original line. Again, the cursor changes to include a curve when you're close enough to the line to make a connection. When you release the mouse button, another new node appears at the release point. The line you've just drawn replaces the portion of the original line between the two new nodes!

Editing Curves

So far, we've covered the most direct ways of drawing, extending, and redrawing lines, using just the line tools. For even finer control, you can use the **Node Tool** and its supporting context toolbar to edit curves (that is our catch-all term for both simple and complex lines). The techniques involved are a bit more complex, but not really more difficult. In fact, the outcome depends less on your eye-hand coordination and more on your having a clear idea of what effect you want. With this tool, you can get just about any effect you desire!

To reshape a curve:

1. Click the **Node Tool** button on the Drawing toolbar.
2. Select any curved line on your page. (Make sure it's a curved line, not a straight line.) The line's nodes appear, and the context toolbar also pops up.

3. Move the cursor over the line. You'll see that when you're over curved segments of the line, it says "SEGMENT." Over a node, the cursor changes to display "NODE."

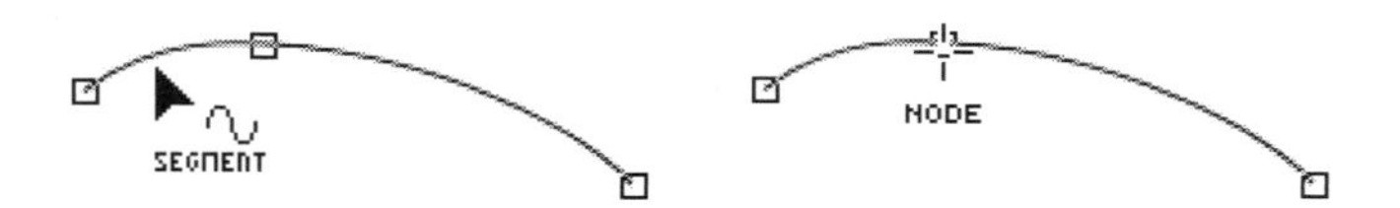

4. Click and drag one of the line's curved segments. The effect is similar to redrawing with the Pencil Tool, except that no new nodes are added—and as long as you hold down the mouse button (showing the Move cursor), you can keep adjusting the shape of the segment until you've got it right.

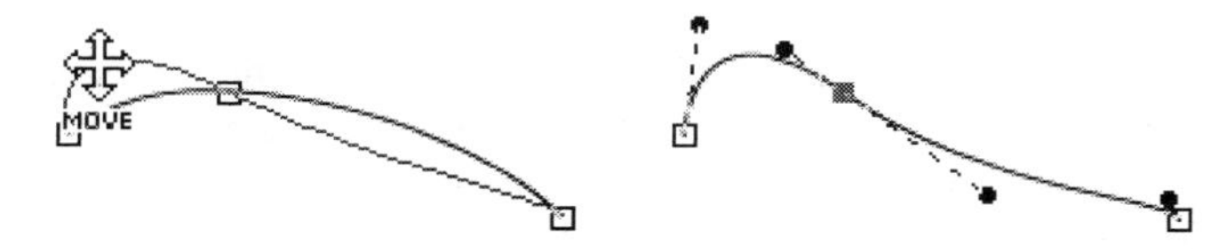

5. Click and drag an "active" red node. By moving a node, you can reposition the curved segments on both sides of the node.

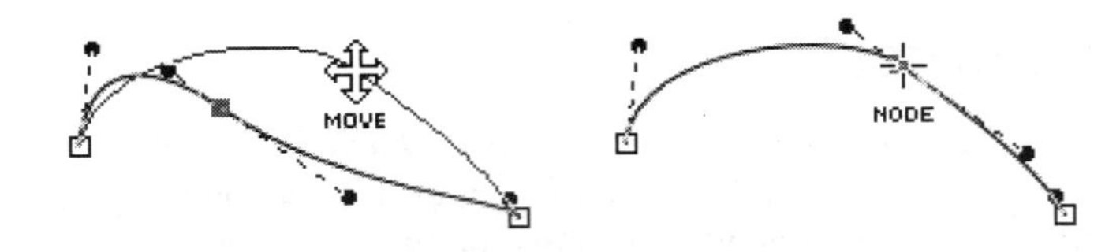

Using control handles

A selected curved segment or a node reveals the **control handles** on adjacent nodes. Each line segment has two control handles, one on either side, that determine the path of the line segment between them. In the case of a very simple curve with only one segment, there are the two handles:

Interior nodes join two segments, and so when you select an interior node you see two handles sticking out from it. Each one helps to control the segment in the direction it's pointing. The following example shows a slightly more complex curve with an interior node selected (at the bottom). You can see that there are two pairs of control handles visible, one for each of the segments joined at the selected node:

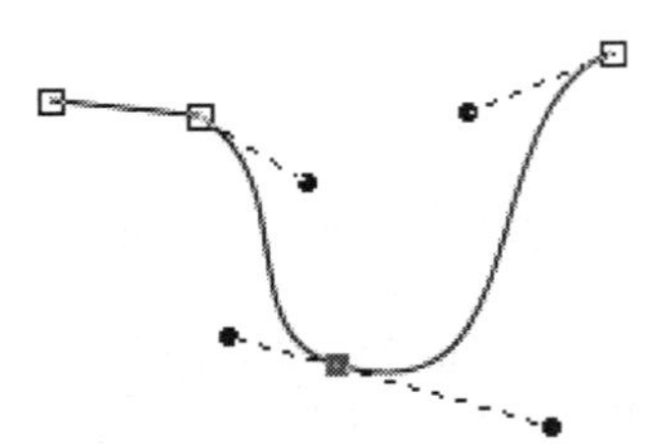

Once you realise that control handles work in pairs like this, it becomes easy to understand how to edit a curve. You can drag a node's control handles independently to produce very precise changes in the curvature of the line on either side. You can shorten or lengthen the handles, which changes the depth of the **curve** (that is, how far out the curve extends), or alter the handle angle, which changes the curve's **slope**.

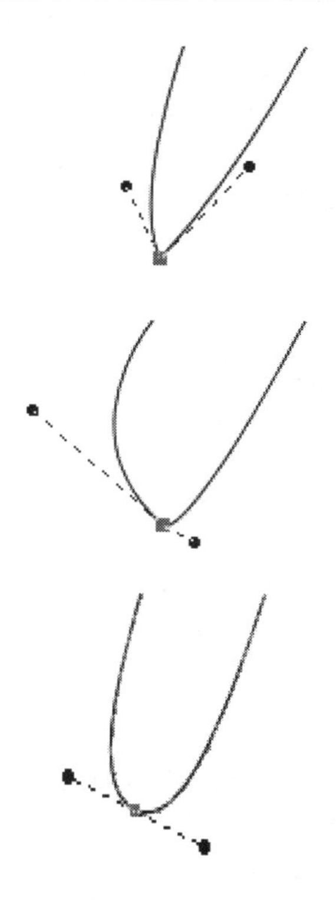

If you look at any particular node, you see its control handles determine how the curve will pass through it. If the two handles are in very different directions then the curve will slope (change direction) sharply as it passes through the node.

If you want a smoother curve then you need to adjust the handles on either side of the node so that the curve leaves the node at the same angle by which it entered. In other words, for a smoother curve the handles have to form a straighter line.

To keep the curvature the same on both sides of the node, the handles also need to be kept at the same length as well as in the same direction.

Fine-tuning a curve

Ready for one more key bit of information about nodes? As we've just seen, when you select an interior node it displays one handle for each of the two line segments joined there. When you adjust one of these handles, how the other responds depends on the node's type. In other words, the node type determines the shape of the junction or corner between two segments.

For line-editing purposes, there are three basic types of corners that you can adjust by hand: **Sharp**, **Smooth**, and **Symmetric**. Then there's a fourth type called **Smart** that applies an automatic curve of its own. Once you've selected a node, you can tell at a glance which type it is by inspecting the context toolbar to see which of the buttons is down. To change the shape of a corner, you simply click a different button—each icon below shows the different corner shapes visually.

A **Sharp** corner means that the lines to either side of the node are completely independent so that the corner can be quite pointed.

A **Smooth** corner means that the slope of the line is the same on both sides of the node, but the depth of the two joined segments can be different.

Symmetric corner nodes join line segments with the same slope and depth on both sides of the node.

Smart nodes automatically determine slope and depth for a rounded, best-fitting curve. If you attempt to adjust a smart corner's handles, it reverts to a symmetric corner. You can always reset the node to smart—but to maintain smart nodes, be careful what you click on!

To turn a curved line segment into a straight line segment:

1. With the **Node Tool**, select the leading node of the line segment (the node nearer the start of the line).
2. Click the **Straighten Line** button on the context toolbar. The selected segment immediately jumps to a straight line.

Conversely, click a straight line segment and then click one of the node corner buttons. Then you can adjust the curvature of the newly created curved segment.

Adding and removing nodes

The **Node Tool** can also be used to add or subtract nodes in the middle of a line.

To add a new interior node:

1. Select a line with the **Node Tool**.
2. With the SEGMENT cursor showing, double-click on the point on the line where you want the node to appear.

Adding a node can be useful if the curve only needs a slight change, because it provides an additional pair of control handles to adjust.

To remove interior node(s):

1. Using the **Node Tool**, select a freeform line that contains your unwanted node(s).
2. Click on a node for deletion (the node turns red).
3. Click the **Delete Node** button on the context toolbar (or press the **Delete** key).

Alternatively, if the line has just been drawn, the **Smoothness** option on the Pencil context toolbar can be used to remove nodes to smooth the curve.

Whatever method is used, when a node is removed, the curve is drawn between the remaining nodes without making any changes to their handles.

Closing, opening, and joining curves

Sometimes you'll want to turn an open curve into a closed curve (a shape, in other words), or you may accidentally misdraw a shape, leaving an open curve. Closing curves involves the automatic drawing of a straight line between the first and last nodes.

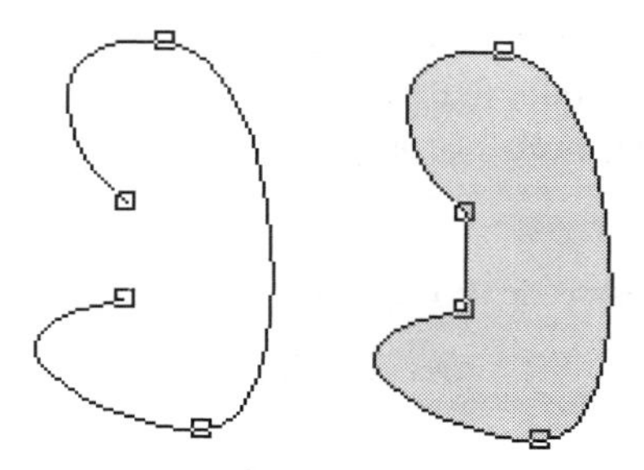

To close a curve:

1. Select a freeform line drawn as an open curve. Use the **Node Tool**.
2. Select the **Close Curve** button from the context toolbar. The closed curve or shape is drawn which can be filled if needed.

If you don't want the curve closed by a straight line, then you can convert the connecting segment's nodes to a smooth or symmetric corner by using the context toolbar.

To join nodes in two separate open curves:

1. Select the two curves you want to join.
2. Choose **Tools>Join Curves**. This adds a straight line between the last and first points of the two curves. The open curve can then be closed as for any other open curve (see above).

To open a curve:

1. With the **Node Tool** selected, pick the node on the closed curve where you want to create the break.
2. Click the **Break Curve** button.
3. Drag each node away from the break point.

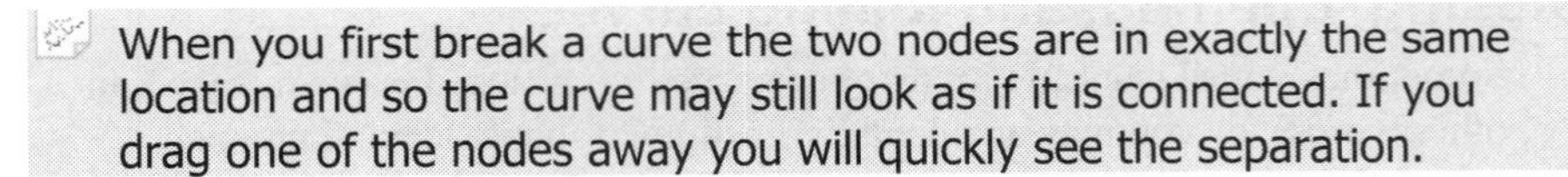
When you first break a curve the two nodes are in exactly the same location and so the curve may still look as if it is connected. If you drag one of the nodes away you will quickly see the separation.

Cleaning curves

For imported vector clipart which, when ungrouped, contains an excessive number of nodes you can removes nodes that aren't needed to determine the shape of the curve. This clean-up is probably only needed if editing the curve.

To clean-up a curve:

- Select the curve and pick **Tools>Clean Curves**. This scans along the curve removing unused nodes to leave a more manageable curve.

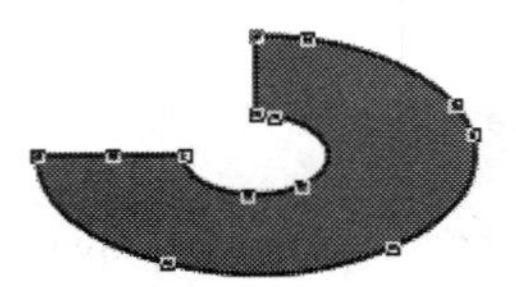

Converting to Curves

Now that you know how to edit a curve, you may wonder how you can do the same things to a QuickShape, or to text for that matter. The problem is that the Node Tool affects a QuickShape or text object quite differently from the way it edits curves. However, converting QuickShapes to curves provides you with a starting point for your own shapes whereas converting text to curves is one way of incorporating letter shapes into designs.

To convert to curves:

1. Select your QuickShape or text object.
2. Choose **Tools>Convert to Curves**.
3. Edit the curve outline using the Node Tool.

The conversion process loses all of its special properties inherent in QuickShapes and text.

Check **Clean Curves** in **Tools>Options>General** to automatically reduce the number of nodes during convert to curve operations—this makes editing a little easier!

Tutorial Resources

For more experience with the tools and techniques covered in this chapter, we recommend these PDF-based tutorials (go to **Help>Tutorials** in DrawPlus):

Try this tutorial...	For practice with these tools and techniques...
Work with Line Tools	Pen tool, Adjusting node handles, Smart segments
Create Shadows and Clouds	Pencil tool
Create a Warped Film Strip	Node Tool

Jump between your PDF tutorials and DrawPlus with **Alt-Tab**.

5
Brushes

Introduction

DrawPlus supports vector and bitmap-warped brushes, the former capable of producing scalable crisp brush strokes, the latter producing natural media effects from acrylic, watercolour, pastel, paint, and charcoal brushes.

An impressive selection of categorized brush presets can be chosen from the **Brushes tab**. Each preset can be edited to your own brush design or copied to a newly created name and category. If you'd like complete control over your brush design, new brushes can be created from scratch.

It's perfectly possible to use any DrawPlus vector object or Bitmap graphic to form the basis of a new brush.

Brush strokes can be applied directly to the page from your mouse or tablet with the latter method ideally suited for applying customizable pressure-sensitive strokes to your drawing. However, painting with the mouse still provides a viable alternative to the tablet. Pressure sensitivity is simulated by use of ready-made customizable pressure profile presets.

Another great benefit of DrawPlus brushes is that there's little chance of spilling paint down yourself and you won't need to clean any brushes afterwards! Let's move on to look at painting and brush use.

How do you Paint?

Painting in DrawPlus inherits the principles of drawing previously described in Drawing Lines on p. 68. The drawing freedom of the Pencil Tool is adapted for brushwork using the dedicated **Paintbrush Tool**. Brush defaults are stored independently of Pencil tool defaults.

You can pick up colour for your brushes as you would for other object, by simply selecting the Paintbrush Tool, choosing your brush type and picking a brush colour from the Colour or Swatches tab.

Using a Pen Tablet

You can either draw with your mouse or, for a more natural experience, use a pen tablet (e.g., Serif GraphicsPad or equivalent).

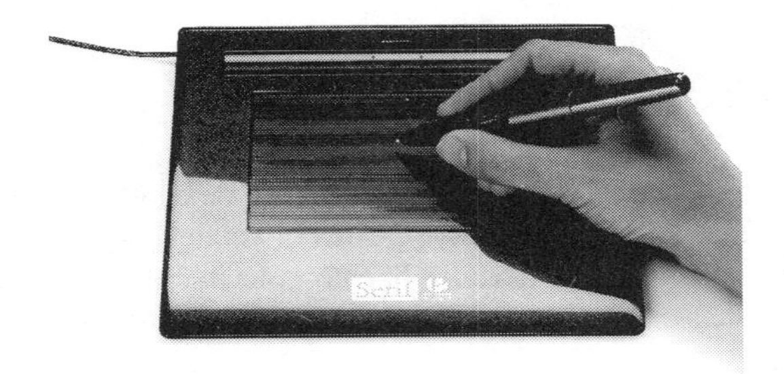

A pen tablet is comprised of an intelligent electronic pad equipped with a pressure-sensitive pen. A rectangular "active" area responds to pressure applied by the pen.

The pad, when connected to your computer, allows realtime drawing within DrawPlus, making the drawing experience as close to a paintbrush as you can get. The tablet's pressure-sensitive pen tip along with DrawPlus itself allows control of stroke width or transparency when painting or drawing—we'll look at pressure sensitivity in more detail on p. 87.

Inspired by a small printed photo or picture? Place the photo directly on top of the tablet and trace its outline(s) with the tablet pen. With the outline(s) stored on a separate layer you can confidently start to paint in the details of another masterpiece!

Using a Mouse

You may have decided that a tablet is not for you. Irrespective, DrawPlus lets you perform all the drawing functions you'll need directly via your mouse. Of course, this is not a pressure-sensitive device in any shape or form but DrawPlus makes sure that pressure sensitivity is simulated as realistically as possible.

Using Brushes

The Brushes tab mentioned previously lets you view brushes currently being used in your document as well as serving as a container for supplied brush presets and your own brush designs. It is possible to edit the existing presets and save your customized brush under a new brush name—even store your own created brushes under your own categories if you'd like to reuse them in different drawings.

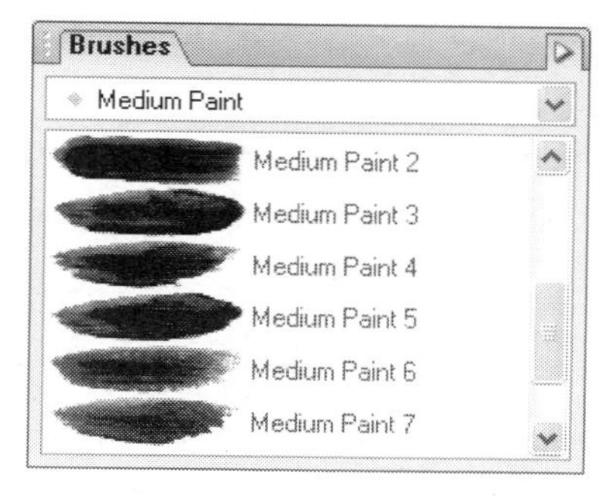

Once you've added your own brush to a category it becomes available in any drawing—simply open the category again, select the brush and paint!

Brush Types

All brushes available from the Brushes tab fall in one of two camps:

- **Stretching**: A standard non-repeating brush where the body is stretched along the length of the brush's body.
- **Repeating**: A repeating brush, as its name suggests, repeats a portion of the brush body over a configurable number of times. Repeating presets are shown with a "_R" name suffix.

See Creating Custom Brushes on p. 87 to see how you create your own brushes.

Using Categories

To make sense of all the brush types available to the user, the preset brushes are stored under a series of pre-defined categories under the name **Global**—the brushes are available to all DrawPlus documents currently open (hence Global!).

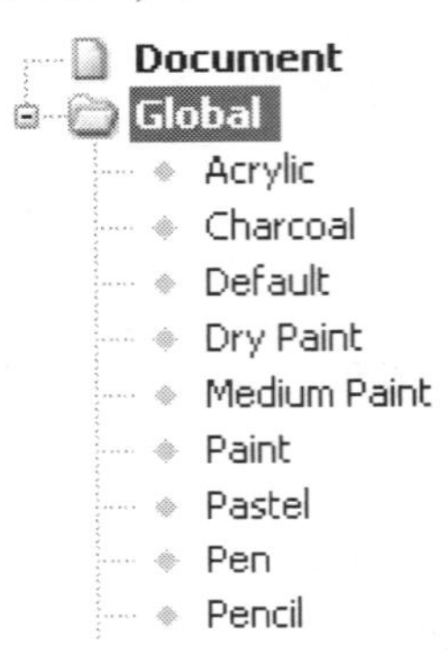

The category names reflect the physical characteristics of the stored brush texture. You can add, rename and reorder any category and even create nested categories within categories.

The **Document** category shows the brush types currently in use in the DrawPlus drawing and is used to store brush types as "bookmarks" for easy reuse in the future.

If you open a friend or colleague's DrawPlus file which contains some very appealing custom brushes, you can always "acquire" them by copying them from the Document category to your own Global category. (See Editing and Copying Brushes on p. 89 or the **Create your Own Brushes** tutorial).

To add, rename or delete Gallery categories:

1. Select the category under which you want to add a new category name.
2. Right-click in the Categories list and choose **Add...**, **Rename...** or **Delete**.
3. For adding and renaming, use the dialog to enter your new category name.

Selecting Brushes

Brush types are hosted as rectangular thumbnail strips in each category of the Brushes tab. Each thumbnail is supported by descriptive text.

Applying Brush Strokes

Using the Paintbrush Tool

The **Paintbrush Tool** is used exclusively to apply brush strokes to the page. The tool is used in conjunction with the **Brushes** tab.

Before going any further it's worth considering how you plan to paint. Like any project a little planning goes a long way!

There are many ways in which people choose to paint, depending on the subject matter, brush type, and the stage of the painting process. The first concern is which brush type, width, and colour will be adopted on application of your first and subsequent brush strokes.

By the way, the displayed Brush cursor indicates that the Paintbrush Tool is selected and that you're ready to Paint!

To apply a brush stroke:

1. Select the **Paintbrush Tool**.
2. Display the Brushes tab and choose a brush from a category.
3. You can either:

- Select a Brush width from the Line tab, a brush colour from the Colour or Swatches tab and finally a level of brush transparency from the Transparency tab.
  OR:
- Select a **Width:**, **Colour...**, or **Opacity:** from the Brush context toolbar.

4. With the brush cursor drag a brush stroke across your page.

The currently displayed settings in the Brush context toolbar (above your workspace) will be adopted for all brush strokes.

After this first brush stroke, there are two ways in which you are likely to paint subsequently, depending on the extent to which you plan to edit brush strokes as you go. To assist you, the **Select on Create** button on the Brushes context toolbar can be used:

- **Edit then Paint**. With the button disabled, the brush stroke is laid down and is immediately deselected. The stroke needs to be reselected to perform any editing. Use when you're happy to set all the brush properties (colour, brush type, width, etc) before painting (as above), especially if you intend to paint repeatedly with the same brush stroke.
- **Paint and Edit**. With the button enabled, a painted brush stroke will remain selected, meaning that the brush stroke can be fine-tuned via the context bar immediately. Use when changing your brush properties frequently, e.g. when adjusting a brush stroke's colour, width, opacity or shape (see Setting Brush Properties on p. 90). The **ESC** key deselects the current brush stroke.

DrawPlus's flexibility still let's you paint and edit without restriction but it's important to know the distinction between the enabled and disabled Select on Create button.

> Trouble applying colour to brush strokes? Remember to select the line swatch on the Colour tab.

Setting Brush Defaults

See Using Object Defaults on p. 60.

Editing Brush Strokes

Any brush stroke laid down can be edited with the supporting dynamic Brushes context toolbar which pops up whenever the Paintbrush Tool is selected. From the context toolbar you can alter the width, colour, opacity and smoothness of the brush stroke amongst others.

As mentioned at the beginning of the chapter, a brush stroke possesses very similar characteristics to a plain line. Therefore, it's not surprising that any brush stroke can be edited, extended or redrawn with the **Node Tool** just as for a straight or curved line (see Chapter 4). The brush stroke path can also be closed or opened.

As a reminder, the selected brush stroke will display it's nodes and segments when the Node Tool is selected. Single or multiple nodes can be deleted, added or dragged around to reshape the brush stroke. You can also fine-tune the brush stroke by dragging the node's control handles as well as changing the node corner type (Straight, Sharp, Smooth, or Symmetric).

Editing and Copying Brushes

At some point, it's more than likely that you will want to edit either an existing preset brush or one you've created yourself. It's possible to edit and overwrite the existing brush preset but it is good practice to copy the brush to you own category (see Using Categories on p. 86) at the same time as you perform brush editing. This prevents your presets from being modified from the originally installed presets. Both copying and editing are carried out by using the Brush Edit dialog.

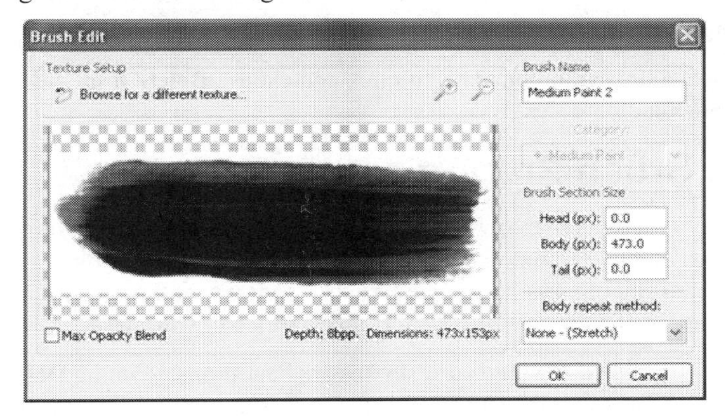

Let's look at both edit and copy methods.

To edit a brush type:

1. Select a brush category from the Brushes tab.
2. Double click on the preview icon of your chosen brush.
3. In the dialog, adjust the head, body or tail in the Brush Section Size. The head and tail can be isolated by either:
   - Setting the **Head (px)** and /or **Tail (px)** values in the Brush Section Size box.
     OR
   - Dragging the left- or right-most blue vertical guides towards the centre of the preview window. Note how the Brush Section Size values change as you adjust each guide.

4. Choose to stretch or repeat the body of a brush by selection from the Body repeat method drop-down menu.
5. Optionally, you can swap the brush texture for another and modify the **Brush Name**. This will rename the existing brush.
6. Click the **OK** button.

This Edit method can only overwrite the existing brush properties. It does not allow you to save the brush type to a new category.

To copy a brush type:

- As for editing a brush type but right-click on the brush preview icon (instead of double clicking) and select **Copy...**. This allows you to save the brush to a new brush name and to the current or a different brush category.

To delete a brush:

- Select a brush thumbnail, right-click and choose **Delete** from the submenu.

Setting Brush Properties

All brushes, irrespective of whether they are vector, Bitmap, repeating or stretching, all have common properties, including brush type, colour, width, opacity, and smoothness. Using the **Brushes context toolbar**, you can adjust the properties of a drawn brush stroke once applied to your page.

Brush types applied to your brush strokes are handily listed in the **Document** folder of the Brushes tab. This useful snapshot is dynamic as it automatically updates if some brush types are no longer used, e.g. if its brush stroke has been deleted.

To change the brush properties of a brush stroke:

1. Select a previously drawn brush stroke this displays the Brushes context toolbar above the workspace.
2. Change the brush design by double-clicking the **Brush:** option, i.e.

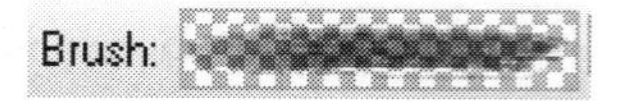

The resulting Brush Edit dialog lets you swap the brush texture, modify the Brush Section Sizes (Head, Tail and Body) and modify the body repeating method for the brush stroke.

This will update all previously applied brush strokes using that brush type. The Brush presets in the Brushes tab will not be affected.

3. Use the **Colour..** button to change the brush stroke colour via a Colour Selector dialog.
4. Alter the brush stroke **Width:** by setting a different point size using the slider (right arrow) or up/down arrows.
5. The overall **Opacity** of the brush stroke can be adjusted using the slider (right arrow) or up/down arrows (100% Opacity represents 0% Transparency; 0% Opacity means 100% Transparency (fully transparent)).

When the Paintbrush Tool is selected rather than a brush stroke, two additional options called **Smoothness** and **Select on Create** are shown on the context toolbar.

1. To set the degree of smoothing to be applied to the brush stroke, set the **Smoothness** value (by entering a value or adjusting the slider).
2. The Select-on-Create button, when enabled, leaves the brush stroke selected on the page or, if disabled, leaves it deselected.

To change brush types:

1. Select the brush stroke.
2. Go to the Brushes tab and select firstly a brush category then a brush type from the displayed qallery. The brush stroke adopts the newly chosen brush.

Creating Custom Brushes

Custom brushes can be created to complement the existing brush presets. The user has the freedom to create new vector or bitmap brushes, based on selected vector objects or bitmaps (e.g., photos), respectively. For all brushes, it is possible to configure differently sized repeat areas and set various repeat methods (2-Part, 3-Part, 4-Part, etc.) for the brush body. This all takes place in a **Brush Edit** dialog.

The only difference between creating a custom brush and editing an existing brush is that for creating brushes the dialog is empty, whereas editing brushes shows the current brush settings in the dialog.

Brush Design

One cast-iron requirement is that you will need a brush design on which to base your brush stroke. A brush design is simply a vector object or Bitmap file which is loaded for the brush type. For Natural Media brushes, each brush preset is bitmap based and is derived from a single .PNG file. Here are some additional guide lines for creating good vector and Bitmap brush designs...

- **File Type**: Any file format can be used, although a format with good bit depth and compression is ideal, e.g. PNG.
- **Shape/Orientation**: The texture should have a rectangular shape with landscape orientation.
- **Resolution**: Pick a resolution of between 1000-5000 pixels wide and 100-300 pixels high.
- **Depth**: For vector graphics, use 8bpp. For bitmap graphics, use 8 or 32bpp. Use 32bpp if Photo brushes are to be used.
- **Colour**: For vector graphics, use colourized graphics, for bitmaps graphics use non-colourized. For transparency, ensure all bitmaps have an alpha channel and that pure white (255,255,255) is used as the background.

Here's an example of a brush design (Water 6) as it would appear in the Brush Edit dialog. It's stored as a PNG file, 3565 x 279 pixels, 8bpp.

Remember that you can edit a current brush as an alternative to starting from scratch.

Setting brush head and tail

Brush designs possess varying characteristics, shape and form. Often you may want to preserve the original texture's start and finish—to do this you delimit the brush texture into discrete portions, i.e. the Head, Body and Tail. This allows the head and tail of the brush to be isolated so they are not subject to stretching or repeating. Consider a picture brush of a friendly "bug"—it's obvious that you'll want to keep the head and tail as is (without stretching or repeating), but equally you'll want to repeat a portion of the brush body to simulate the insect's body segments (shown as the light area between the vertical guide lines).

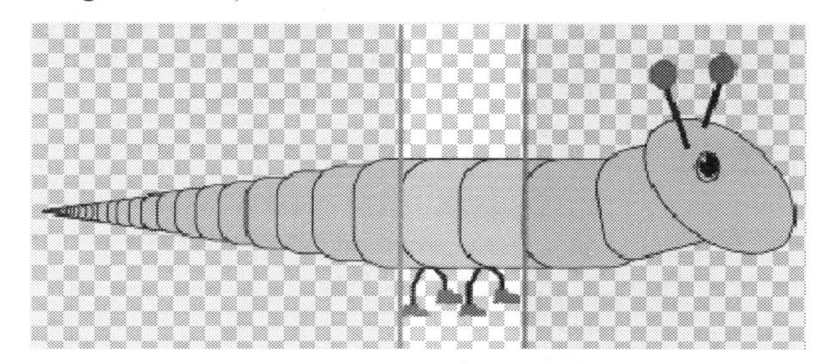

Try not to make the Body section of the brush too long—either split the brush head, body and tail into three equal portions or make the body section 2-Part repeating.

Stretching vs. Repeating

The way a brush stroke is applied is fundamentally based on the stretching or repetition of the middle portion of the brush. Whichever you use depends on the brush design you are working with and the effect you want to achieve. Drawplus supplies both stretching and repeating brush designs equally.

Natural media brushes, as bitmap brushes, can be stretched or repeated depending on the texture. For example, a **Charcoal 22** texture would look odd if stretched because it has a naturally granular appearance. Compare this to a paint texture, e.g. Medium Paint 1, where the regular horizontal grain can be stretched without compromising the brush design. If you use a photo as your brush design it's pretty clear that a repeating element is needed rather than stretching the photo throughout the brush stroke.

Now we've looked at brush design, a brush's structure and how it can be applied, we'll now look at creating, editing and copying brush types.

Creating Bitmap Brushes

To add a new Bitmap Brush:

1. Display the Brushes tab, then right-click in the gallery window and select **Add...**.
2. In the Brush Edit Dialog, pick a new brush name and brush category (pick one from the drop-down menu).
3. Use the **Browse for a different texture** button to locate then select a bitmap which will be the texture of your new brush.
4. Under Brush Section Size, change values in the **Head (px)**, **Body (px)** and **Tail (px)** input boxes or by dragging the blue vertical guides in the brush preview window.
5. The light area (between the vertical guides) in the brush preview window can be either stretching or repeating. In the **Body repeat method** section, select a stretch (**None - (Stretch)**) or repeating method (**Simple** or **2-Part**, **3-Part**, etc.) from the drop-down menu.

Creating Vector Brushes

To add a new Vector Brush:

1. Select an object in your DrawPlus drawing.
2. In the Tools menu, select **Create Vector Brush...**.
3. In the dialog, enter a brush name and select an existing category in which to store the new vector brush.

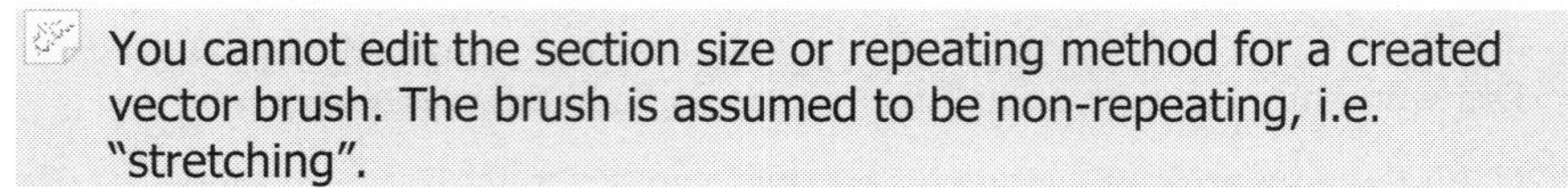

You cannot edit the section size or repeating method for a created vector brush. The brush is assumed to be non-repeating, i.e. "stretching".

Applying Pressure Sensitivity

Along with a brushes natural characteristics (its bristles, shape, and size), pressure sensitivity also plays a major part in how a brush is applied to your page. The extent to which a brush is applied is at the heart of an artist's creative ability. A heavily applied brush could help to convey strong imagery (e.g., moods), whereas a brush applied more lightly may indicate a more subtle effect.

In DrawPlus's world we apply pressure by using a pressure-sensitive device (a tablet and pen) and control how that pressure affects your brush stroke in DrawPlus's **Pressure** tab.

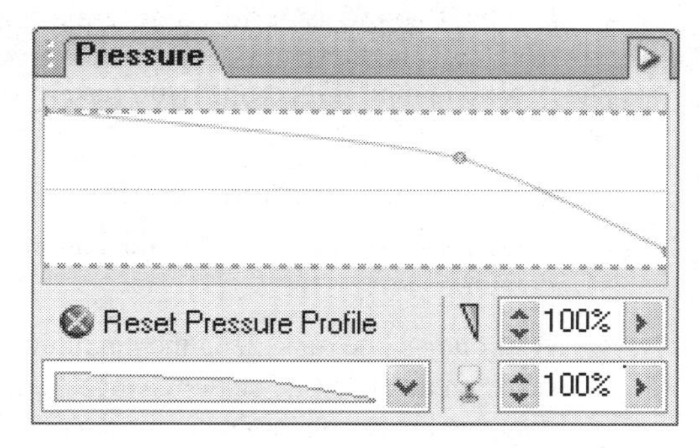

This tab is used to apply different pressure profile presets, create your own profiles from scratch and adjusts how the brush's width and transparency changes in response to pressure. The maximum and minimum pressure can also be controlled via the tab—your brush strokes can appear more subtle or striking as a result (see Adjusting Pressure Variance on p. 98).

The pressure chart may appear a little daunting at first! It becomes a lot clearer if you imagine the chart when it is superimposed over the brush itself—it represents one half of a brush stroke along its entire length. Of course, the same profile shape will be mirrored on the lower half of the stroke exactly.

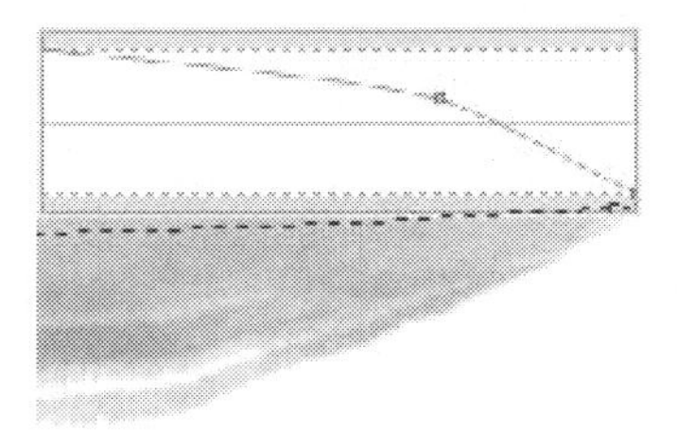

To apply a pressure profile:

1. Expand the **Pressure** tab at the bottom of your screen, and choose a pressure profile from the drop-down menu.

   The pressure chart updates to reflect the chosen profile.

2. Apply a brush stroke to the page. This will adopt the chosen pressure profile.

The profile is maintained until you reset it or pick another profile from the preset list.

To create a new pressure profile:

1. Click the **Reset Pressure Profile** button. This sets the pressure chart back to default.
2. A turquoise line runs along the maximum pressure line at the top of the chart. Click on this line (the cursor changes) and drag downwards, moving the displayed red node into your chosen position. You now have a blue curve which represents the pressure profile.
3. Repeat the process for the number of nodes that you want to add to make up the profile.

TIP: Edit an existing pressure profile from the preset drop-down menu to create profiles quickly.

You can then save the current pressure settings to your own saved pressure profile—this allows you to store and reapply your settings at any point in the future.

To save a new pressure profile:

1. In the Pressure tab, change the profile as described above.
2. Click on the **Options** button and select **Add Pressure Profile**.

Your new profile is automatically added to the bottom of the pressure profile preset drop-down list.

To delete a pressure profile:

1. Click on the **Options** button and select **Manage Pressure Profiles...**.
2. In the dialog, select the pressure profile for deletion and click the **Delete** button.

Altering Brush Width and Opacity with Pressure

For subtle brush pressure control, DrawPlus can vary the extent to which pen pressure can alter a brush's original width and opacity. This is expressed as a percentage of the original brush **Width** and **Opacity** values shown in the Brushes context toolbar. Imagine the end of your brush stroke tapering off or getting fainter as it lifts off the page—the concept is simple!

You can set the degree to which width and opacity changes either independently or in combination. Let's look at some examples... based on a **Default** brush called Circle. The example doesn't use a natural media texture so the concept is illustrated more clearly. We'll use a pressure profile available from the preset drop-down menu for all examples.

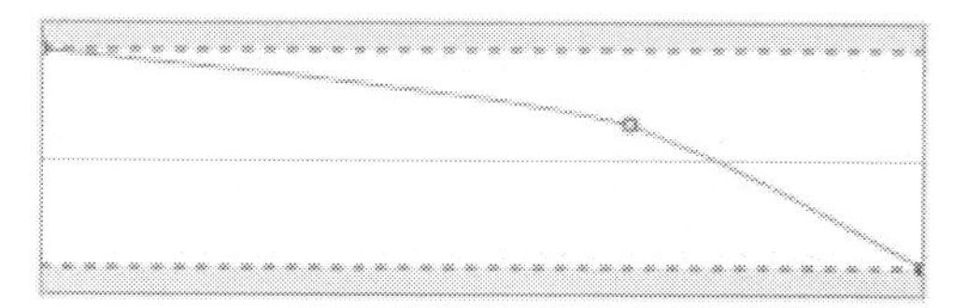

Here's how the degree of width/opacity changes the brush stroke appearance.

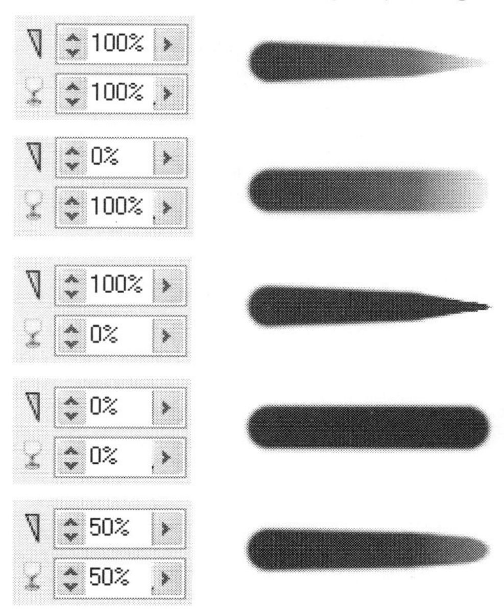

The first example shows the default behaviour when brush pressure is applied.

These settings are adjusted independently and are not stored with the pressure profiles.

To adjust brush width with pressure:

1. Select a previously drawn brush.
2. In the **Pressure** tab, pick a pressure profile from the drop-down menu.
3. Enter a **Width** value by setting a percentage value in the input box, using the slider or using the up/down arrows. The lower the value the less the pressure effects the brush width, i.e. a value of 50% will apply half the brush width under pressure.

To adjust opacity with pressure:

1. Select a previously drawn brush.
2. In the **Pressure** tab, pick a pressure profile from the drop-down menu.
3. Enter an **Opacity** value by setting a percentage value in the input box, using the slider or using the up/down arrows. The lower the value the pressure effects the brush opacity, i.e. a value of 50% will apply half the brush opacity under pressure.

Adjusting Pressure Variance

A useful DrawPlus feature is the ability to set the degree to which pressure is applied via your brush stroke—this is called the **pressure variance**. This variance is controlled by setting a maximum and/or minimum pressure and acts independently of the effect of brush pressure on brush width and opacity. The variance is set within the pressure chart of the Pressure tab.

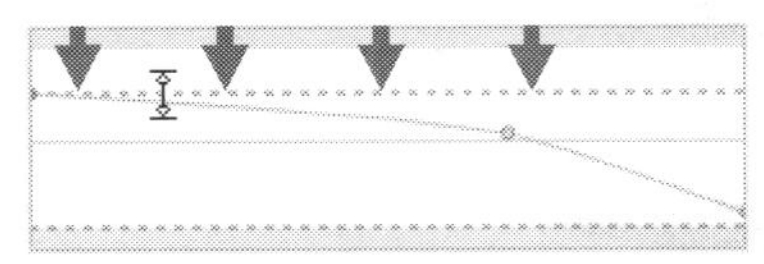

Reducing maximum pressure

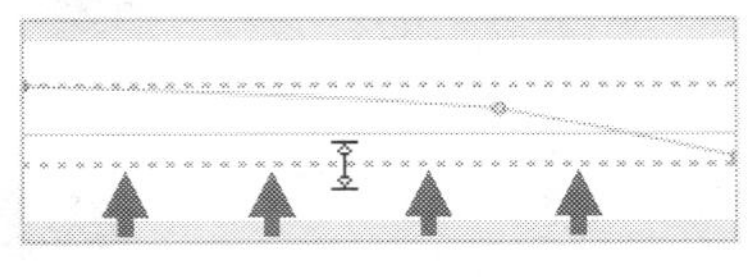

Increasing minimum pressure (after reducing max. pressure)

To reduce maximum pressure:

1. Display the Pressure tab.
2. Select a pressure profile from the drop-down menu (modifying the profile by adjusting nodes if necessary).
3. Hover the cursor over the upper dashed line in the pressure chart. Click and drag the line downwards while holding the mouse down. Release to set a new reduced maximum pressure setting. Note how the profile is compressed into the remaining chart area.

To increase minimum pressure:

- As for reducing the maximum pressure but drag the lower dashed line upwards to raise the minimum pressure setting.

Tutorial Resources

For more experience with the tools and techniques covered in this chapter, we recommend these PDF-based tutorials (go to **Help>Tutorials** in DrawPlus):

Try this tutorial...	For practice with these tools and techniques...
Use the Natural Media Brushes	Using Brushes tab, Paintbrush Tool, Brush Context toolbar, and Pressure tab. Apply and edit brush strokes using the mouse and pen tablet. Change brush stroke attributes. Adjust the pressure-sensitivity and pressure profile of your brush strokes.
Make Your Own Brushes	Create brush categories, vector and bitmap brushes. Copy and edit brushes. Create stretching and repeating bitmap brushes from a photo and scanned image.

Jump between your PDF tutorials and DrawPlus with **Alt-Tab**.

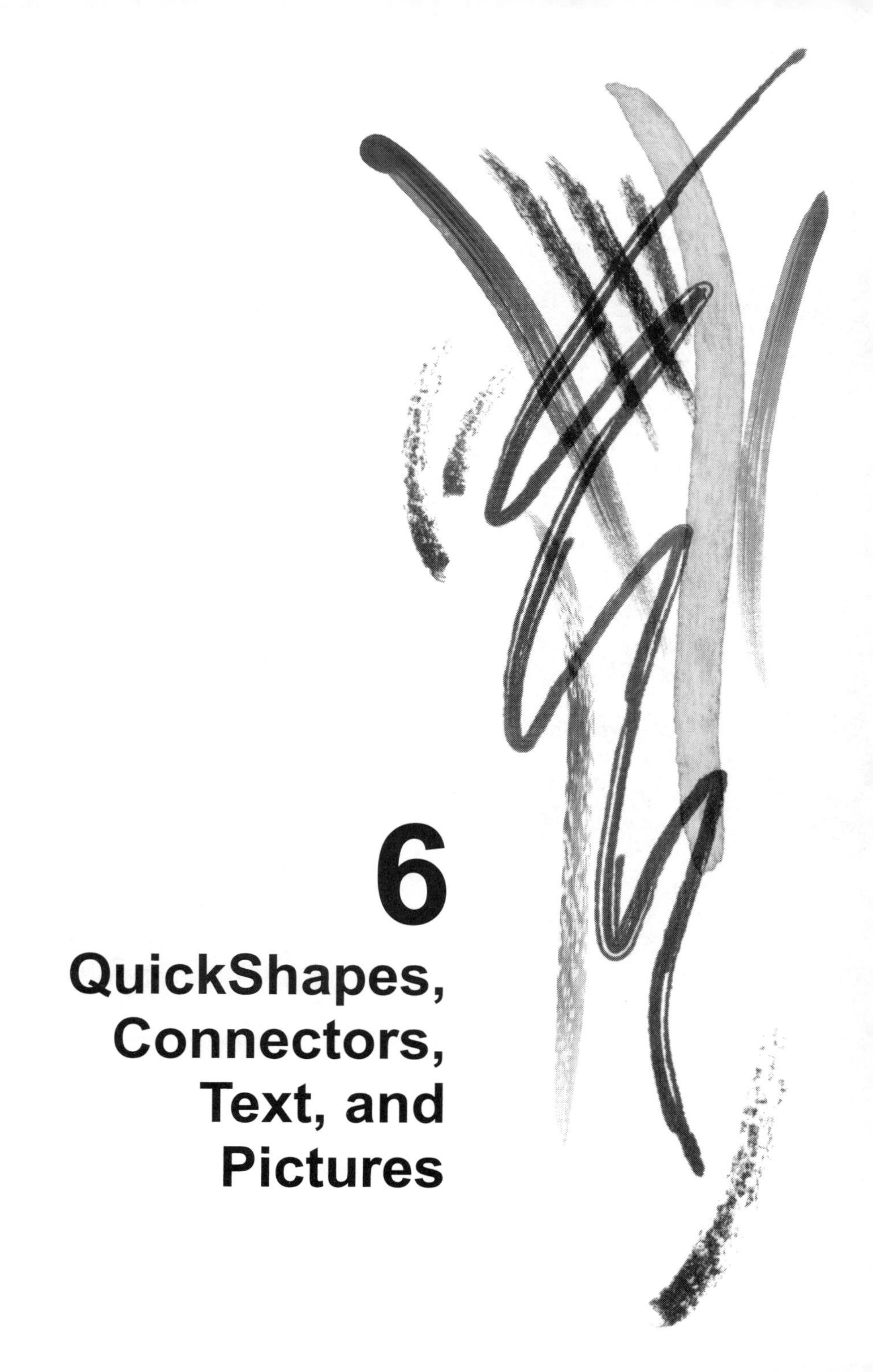

6

QuickShapes, Connectors, Text, and Pictures

Introduction

This chapter will focus particularly on QuickShapes, connectors and text objects—and explore a variety of ways to customize them. In addition, we'll take a quick look at how DrawPlus handles bitmap pictures.

QuickShapes

QuickShapes are pre-designed objects that you can instantly add to your page, then adjust and vary using control handles.

QuickShapes are added from a flyout containing a wide variety of commonly used shapes, including boxes, arrows, hearts, spirals and other useful symbols.

Once you've drawn your QuickShape, you can adjust its properties—for example, apply solid, gradient or Bitmap fills (including your own bitmap pictures!) or apply transparency effects. You can even use the **sliding handles** to create variations on the original QuickShape.

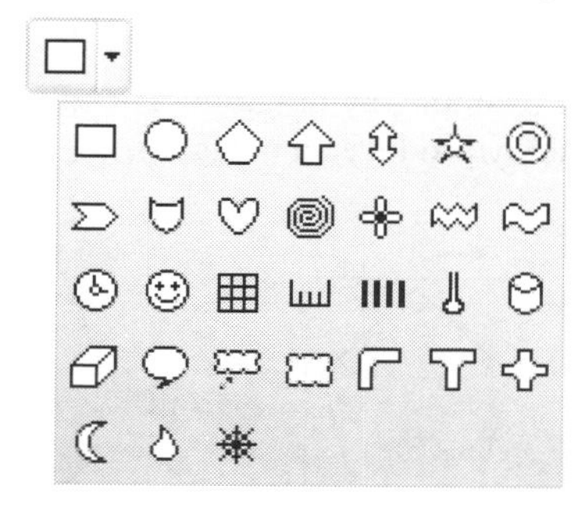

It's also possible to use the always-at-hand Quickshape context toolbar situated above the workspace to swap QuickShapes, and adjust a QuickShape's line weight, colour and style.

To create a QuickShape:

1. Click the **QuickShape** button on the Drawing toolbar and select a shape from the QuickShape flyout. The button takes on the icon of the shape you selected.
2. Click on the page to create a new shape at a default size. New QuickShapes adopt the currently set line and fill in DrawPlus.
3. To resize, select with the Pointer Tool, drag a selection handle and release the mouse button at the new size.

To draw a constrained shape (such as a circle):

- Hold down the **Ctrl** key as you drag.

All QuickShapes can be positioned, resized, rotated, and filled. What's more, you can adjust their designs using the Node Tool. Each shape changes in a logical way to allow its exact appearance to be altered. The ability to alter the appearance of QuickShape objects makes them more flexible and convenient than clipart pictures with similar designs.

To adjust the appearance of a QuickShape:

1. Select it with the **Node Tool**. One or more sliding handles appear next to the shape. Different QuickShapes have different handles.
2. To find out what each handle does for a particular shape, move the Node Tool over the handle and read the HintLine.
3. To change the appearance of a QuickShape, drag its handles.

For example, by dragging a handle to the left on the pentagon below will quickly produce an octagon:

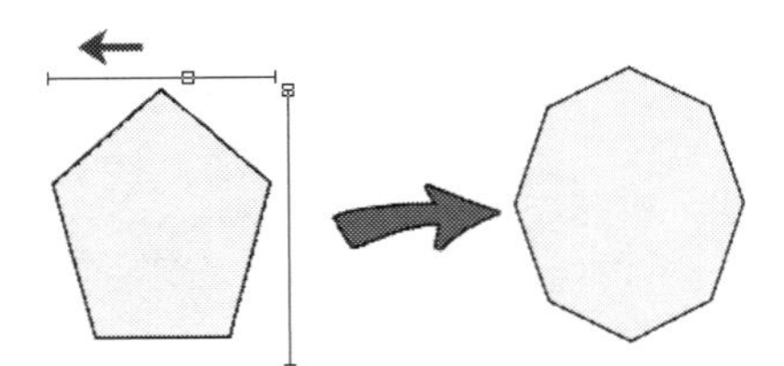

Some QuickShapes have more than two handles. For example, the Quick Star has four, which allow you to create everything from a traditional five-pointed star to a crazy star shape!

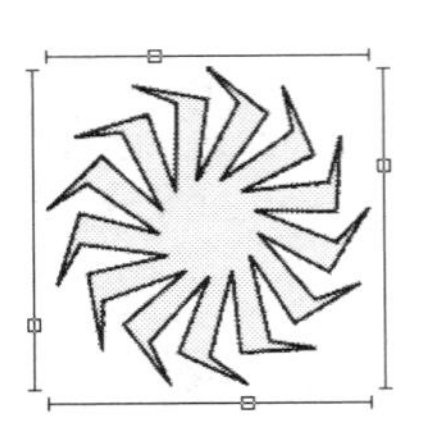

Connectors

Connectors are special lines that you can anchor to objects, where they remain attached even if one or both objects are moved or resized. Using connectors, you can easily create dynamic diagrams and charts that show relationships, such as family trees, organization charts, and flow charts. If you need to rearrange the elements, the connections are preserved.

The **Connector Tool**, when selected, offers various connector tool options on the Connectors context toolbar situated above the workspace.

- The **Direct Connector** tool option draws a single, straight-line connector between any two connection points.
- The **Right Angle Connector** tool option creates connectors that use one vertical and one horizontal segment so the connector shape is a right angle. These are great for keeping your organization charts simple.
- The **Auto Connector** tool option is an adaptable connector that intelligently adjusts its shape to route around "obstructive" objects—perfect for complex diagrams with interwoven pathways.

The context toolbar also adjusts a Connector's line weight, line end, colour and style.

To connect objects via connectors:

1. Select the **Connector Tool** on the Line Tools flyout (Drawing toolbar). Hover over an object so that default **connection points** become visible. For example on the leftmost Quick Rectangle:

2. From the displayed context toolbar, select the **Direct Connector** tool option.

3. Click the connection point on the right edge midpoint of the left shape. Drag to the right and release the mouse button when the pointer is over the connection point on the left edge midpoint of the right shape. (You'll see a box appear around the point when a connection is imminent.) A direct connector will appear between the two connection points.

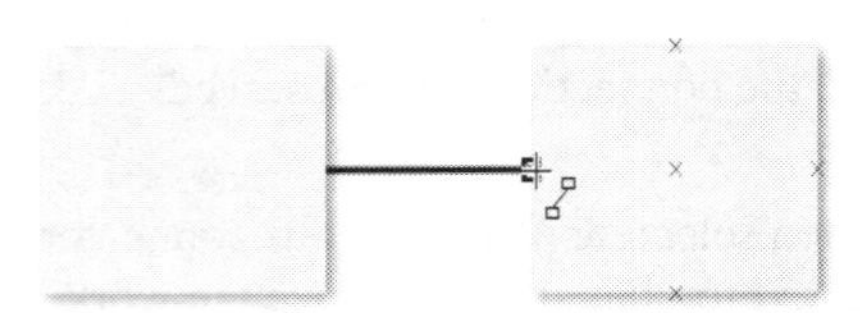

4. Select the right-hand shape and drag to a new position with the **Pointer Tool**; the connection points vanish, but the connector remains. The connector follows!

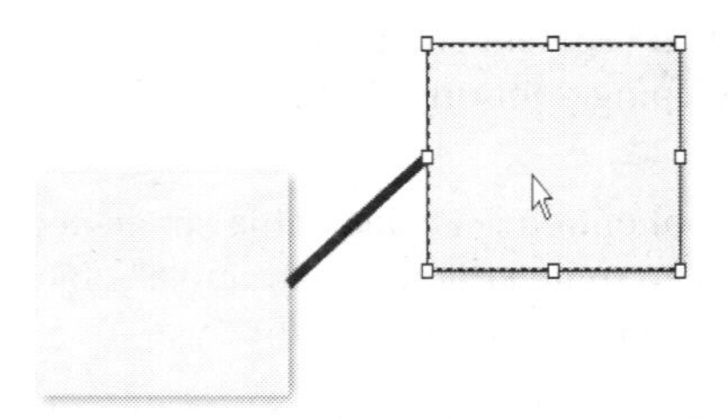

We could have attached either end of the connector to any of the visible connection points, or even kept it free-floating (in which case it would be anchored to a point on the page).

To switch between different connector types:

- Right-click on the connector, choose **Connectors** and select a new connector type to convert to from the menu. The connector is redrawn automatically.

To change connector points by Auto Selection:

1. Select the connector with the **Node Tool**.
2. Drag one of the end nodes over a different Auto Select connection point on the object. These points are visible and allow the connector to snap into position. Release when the small box appears, and the connector re-anchors.

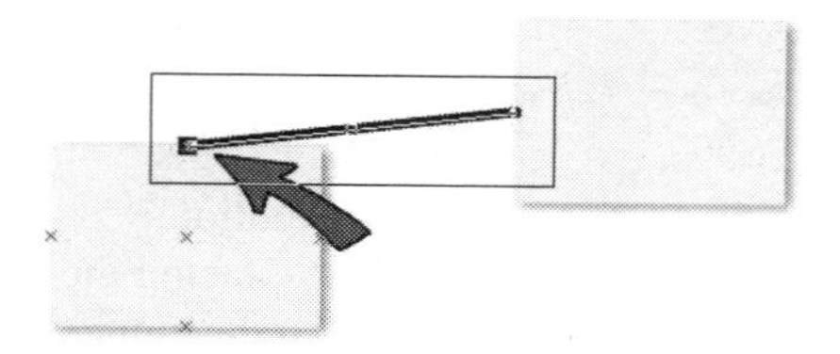

It's called the **Auto Select** connection point because a connector which was anchored there will always draw using the connection point that results in the shortest connector, i.e. the one nearest to the other object.

What if you want to anchor a connector to a specific (custom) point on an object, but it's *not* one of the default Auto Select connection points? That's where the **Connection Point** tool option comes in handy.

To create custom connection points:

1. Click the **Connector Tool** on the Line Tools flyout (Drawing toolbar) again.
2. Select the **Connection Point** tool option on the context toolbar. The Auto Select connection points appear in red on a selected object.
3. Click somewhere in the interior of the shape and a blue custom connection point appears. You can add custom connection points anywhere but typically you will want them positioned around the perimeter of an object—to do this hold the **Ctrl** key down when you click.

You can select and move custom connection points with the Connection Point tool. To delete one, simply select it and press **Delete**. Otherwise, they function basically like default Auto Select connection points, i.e. they can be connected to identically.

Using Auto Connectors

Auto connectors will automatically choose the best route for a particular path between connectors, given the objects' placement and the connection points you've chosen. They will redraw to a new shape whenever any objects are moved or resized. The shape it assumes will use as many line segments as necessary and will even route around objects that are placed in the way of the original connector. They use horizontal and vertical line segments only.

As an example of their use, consider a simple design problem and solution for an organization chart.

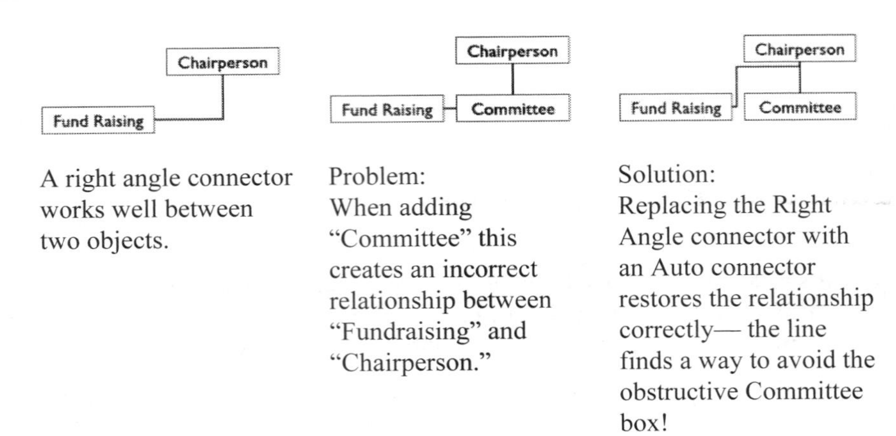

A right angle connector works well between two objects.

Problem:
When adding "Committee" this creates an incorrect relationship between "Fundraising" and "Chairperson."

Solution:
Replacing the Right Angle connector with an Auto connector restores the relationship correctly— the line finds a way to avoid the obstructive Committee box!

To Auto Connect between connection points:

1. Draw two objects.
2. Click the **Connector Tool** on the Line Tools flyout (Drawing toolbar).
3. Select the **Auto Connector** tool option. Default connection points will appear when hovering over any selected object(s).
4. Hover over on a connection point and drag to another connection point, typically on a different object. Release when the small box appears, and the connector re-anchors.

> Remember that you can change your Direct or Right Angle connectors to be Auto Connectors at any time if you are not happy with connector positioning.

Auto connectors are intelligent in another way: they know when they've crossed one another, and form "bridges" as needed to keep the connector lines separate, as shown here:

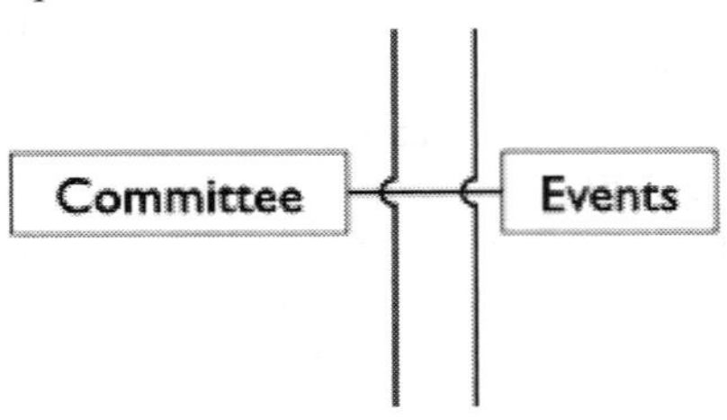

The **Layout** pane of the **Tools>Options...** dialog includes settings that let you adjust the allowed separation between Auto connectors and page objects, as well as the size and spacing of bridges. (Search "connectors" in the DrawPlus Help Index.)

Editing connector properties

You can edit connector properties like thickness, colour, and line ending just like those of standard lines (see Fill, Line, and Transparency Effects on p. 123). And you can edit the shape of connectors using the Node Tool (again just like regular lines, as covered in the previous chapter) if a different shaped path is desirable. Reshaped connectors become "Custom Connectors," losing their Auto properties so you may need to adjust the route to avoid other objects.

Text

There are two kinds of text used in DrawPlus—standalone **free text** and contained **shape text**—both created and edited with the **Text Tool**. As with other objects, it's easy to edit text after you've created it, in this case by retyping or altering properties like font, style, and point size. Beyond that, you can manipulate text objects like other graphic objects.

Each type of text has its own advantages.

Free text

Free text behaves more independently than Shape Text and its individual letters have both line and fill properties.

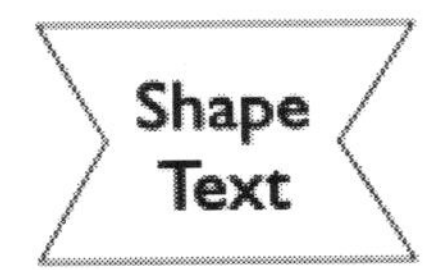

Shape text lacks a line property, but it conforms to the containing shape, and you can achieve unique **text flow** effects by varying the container's properties.

To create free text on the page:

1. Select the **A** **Text Tool** from the Drawing toolbar.
2. Either:

- Click once on page, the blinking cursor will display at the default text size.
  OR
- Click and drag to resize the text cursor to your preferred text size before you type.

3. Type directly onto the page.

To create Shape text on the page:

1. Create a shape from the QuickShape flyout.
2. Start typing, and text will flow into the shape. If you alter the shape later, the text will assume new contours as well.

TIP: You can extract shape text from its container as free text by right-clicking the shape and choosing **Detach as New Object>Text**. Then choose the Pointer Tool and drag off the newly separated text.

With either type of text, if you press the **Enter** key while typing, you can type multiple lines of text as a single object.

Sample Text
This is a sample of
multiline text

If you've typed more text into a shape than it can display, a plus symbol appears below the shape when it's selected. To reveal all the text, you can either enlarge the shape or reduce the size of the text.

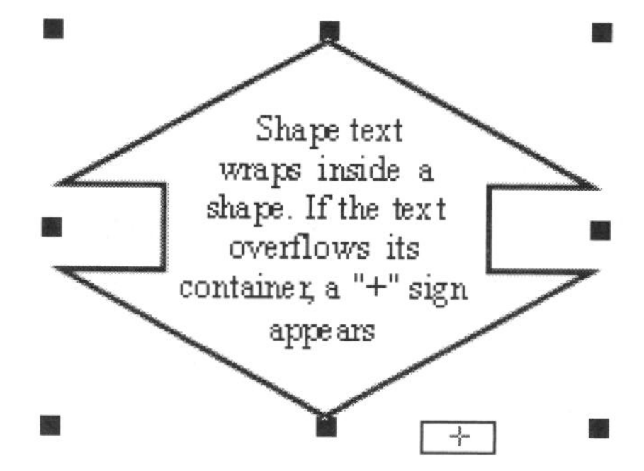

Once you have finished entering either type of text you can switch to one of the three selection tools and the object will be selected with handles. Then you can modify it just like any other graphics object. You can scale, rotate, skew, move, and copy it, and apply fills, line styles, and transparency, as well as a wide variety of Special Effects (see p. 177).

Text properties

The actual text of DrawPlus text objects has the same attributes you would expect to find in any standard word processor—including font, point size, style, line colour, fill colour, line weight, letter spacing, line spacing (leading), and alignment.

New text automatically takes on the default properties (see p. 60) for either free text or shape text. The two are defined separately, with shape text defaults subsumed under other shape properties. To set new defaults, create a sample object with the desired attributes, then right-click it and choose **Update Defaults** or set **Synchronize Defaults** on the Standard toolbar (see p. 60).

Selecting text

You can select either kind of text right on the page using the Text Tool, and then retype or reformat it. The displayed Text context toolbar provides convenient access to several basic attributes. The point size drop-down list shows the vertical size of the selected text in points. (The point is a traditional measure of the size of text; there are 72 points to the inch.)

The Text context toolbar displays a WYSIWYG listing of available fonts, and you can apply any font simply by selecting from the list when a text object has been previously selected!

Resizing text

To resize text with context toolbar:

- Select the text and pick a different 24.0 pt **Font size** from the context toolbar.

OR

- Select the free text then drag any selection handle. Use the **Ctrl** key to maintain the text's aspect ratio, otherwise text can be distorted to great effect!

You can also specify whether shape text will or won't scale in proportion when its containing shape is resized. Right-click on the shape, select **Text>Text Flow** from the menu and check the **Scale text with Object** option.

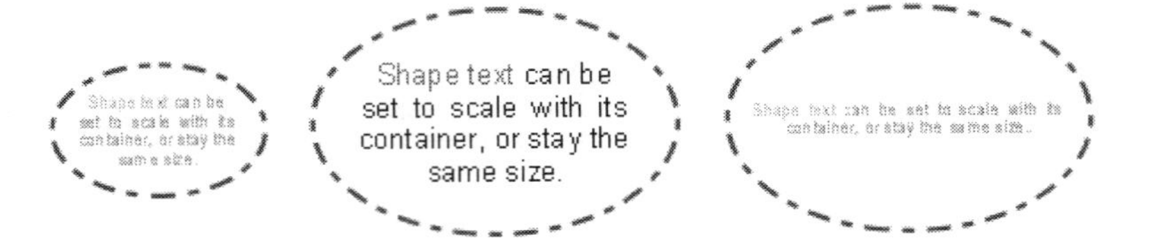

To change text alignment:

- Select **Align Left**, **Align Centre**, **Align Right**, or **Justify** from the Standard toolbar to let you align text objects with multiple lines.

To change font styles:

1. Select your text.
2. Choose a **B** **Bold** and/or *I* **Italic** font style from the Standard toolbar.

To change tracking, leading, and wrapping on free text:

- Select a text object with the **Node Tool**. The object displays three control handles to the left, top and bottom of the text (this won't work for shape text).
    - To set (space between characters), drag the handle (shown as LETTER) located below the text.

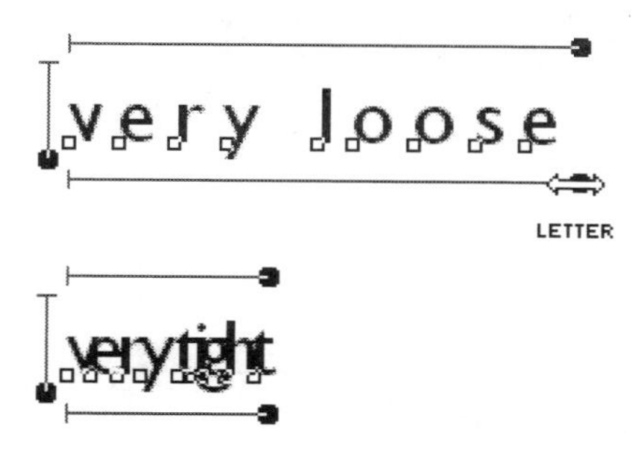

- To set leading (space between lines), drag the handle located to the left of the text (will be shown as LEADING).
- To set wrapping (how line wraps onto a new line), drag the handle located above the text (will be shown as WRAP).

To change text indents and vertical spacing:

1. Right-click a text object and choose **Text**. You'll see a submenu with choices—select **Paragraph...**.
2. The paragraph dialog lets you adjust the left, right and first line indents. For vertical spacing set a percentage leading or add space above/below your text.

To change text flow properties:

Text flow properties include **vertical alignment** and **wrap**, which determine how lines of either free text or shape text are positioned in relation to the object boundaries.

1. Right-click a text object and choose **Text**. You'll see a submenu with choices—select **Text Flow...**.
2. Enter an amount, from the left, right, top and bottom, that text should be indented from the shape's boundaries.

Online help includes a complete listing of text properties in the "Editing text" topic.

The Edit Text window

For managing large amounts of text (for example, shape text that has overflowed its container), the Edit Text window affords a simple word processing environment.

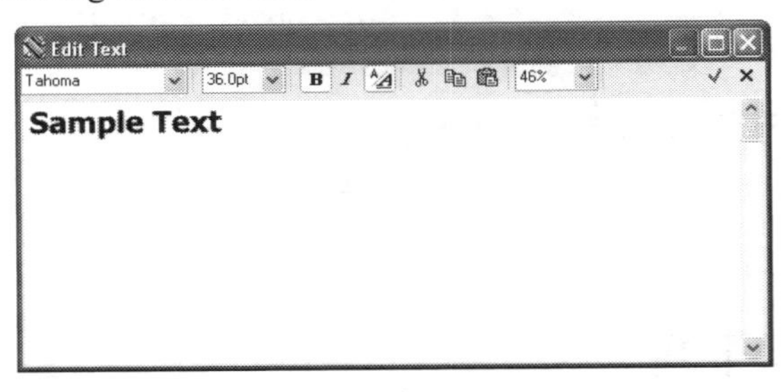

To edit text in Edit Text window:

1. Double-click a free text object with the Pointer Tool, or right-click a shape text object and choose **Text>Edit Text**.
2. Apply different attributes: font, point size, bold, and italic. Select the letters or words you want to change with the cursor, and then use the buttons on the toolbar to apply properties to it.
3. To return to DrawPlus, click the ✓ **OK** button to update, or ✗ **Cancel** button to abandon changes.

> Click the **Show Formatting** button to switch between unformatted (draft) and formatted view—use the unformatted view for editing lots of text at once.

Unicode text

On occasion, you may wish to import text in a foreign language, e.g. to include a foreign quote in its original language. To work outside the standard ASCII character set, DrawPlus allows Unicode characters to be pasted (using **Edit>Paste Special...**) from the clipboard into your drawing.

To retain formatting, use "*Formatted Text (RTF)*" or for plain text use "*Unformatted Unicode Text*". For the latter, if imported text appears as blocks instead, remember to apply a Unicode font such as Arial Unicode MS to fix the formatting.

Special text effects

We'll be looking at fill and transparency in the next chapter, and we'll deal with other special effects such as shadows, filter effects, perspective, text art, enveloped and curved text in Special Effects starting on p. 177.

Pictures

DrawPlus lets you insert pictures from a wide variety of file formats. Here's a quick overview:

- **Bitmapped** pictures, also known as **bitmaps** or **raster** images, are built from a matrix of dots ("pixels"), rather like the squares on a sheet of graph paper. They may originate as digital camera photos or scanned images, or be created (or enhanced) with a "paint" program or photo editor. Convert to a DrawPlus graphic with autotrace.
- **Draw** graphics, also known as **vector** graphics are resolution-independent and contain drawing commands such as "draw a line from A to B." These are like DrawPlus drawings, made of many individual objects grouped together, and you can edit them in the same sort of way. You have the choice of ungrouping the objects in order to edit them further, or leaving them as a group.
- **Metafiles** are the native graphics format for Windows and combine raster and vector information.

Any imported picture ends up as an object you can select, move, scale, shear, rotate—and even crop using the **Envelope Tool** on the Drawing toolbar.

You can also acquire images directly from PhotoCDs or via TWAIN devices (scanners or digital cameras).

DrawPlus has full support for making image adjustments to either correct deficiencies in the original photo or to apply a special effect, enhancing the visual appeal of the image.

Pictures as fills

You can add bitmaps to the Bitmap fill gallery of the Swatches tab by importing the picture into the DrawPlus gallery directly. The swatch can then be used as a fill for other objects (see Gradient/bitmap Fills on p. 131).

Importing pictures

To manually import an image from a file:

1. Click the **Import Picture** button on the Drawing toolbar.
2. Use the **Insert Picture** dialog to browse files and select the file to import, then click **Open**. The dialog disappears and the mouse pointer changes to the Picture Size cursor. What you do next determines the initial size, placement, and aspect ratio (proportions) of the image.
3. Either:

- To insert the picture at a default size, simply click the mouse.
  OR
- To set the size of the inserted picture, drag out a region and release the mouse button.

Normally, the picture's aspect ratio is preserved. To allow free dragging to any aspect ratio, hold down the **Shift** key. To constrain the aspect ratio to a square, hold down the **Ctrl** key.

To import pictures from a digital camera or TWAIN device (scanner):

1. Set up your digital device for image acquisition by following the instructions supplied with the device.
2. If you have multiple TWAIN-compatible devices, choose the device from which your image will be acquired—**Picture>TWAIN>Select Source** from the Insert menu lets you select your device from a menu.
3. For scanning or photo import, choose **Picture>TWAIN>Acquire** from the Insert menu to open the device's image management dialog. Follow the device manufacturer's instructions, and select the scanned image or photo for import.
4. In DrawPlus, the Picture Size cursor is displayed which allows image/photo to be placed at default size (by single-click) or sized (by dragging across the page).

You can also use "autotracing" to import a bitmap as a vector graphic. Choose **Picture>Autotrace...** from the Insert menu and select the file to import. You can adjust smoothness and tolerance settings while previewing the resulting image in the dialog prior to importing.

Image Adjustments

The **Picture context toolbar** appears automatically when you select an imported picture on the page. You can use the bar to improve the appearance of any image appearing in your document by adjusting contrast, brightness, colour, and size directly, or by applying **Image adjustments**.

DrawPlus comes equipped with a comprehensive mix of colour correction/ adjustment tools for use on your newly imported images. Levels, Colour Balance, Channel Mixer, Dust and Scratch Remover and Hue/Saturation/Lightness corrective adjustments, amongst others, are available. Effect-inducing adjustments also range from the artistic Diffuse Glow to various blurring effects. In fact, over 20 adjustments can be directly applied to your image not only individually but cumulatively.

Adjustments are managed by using the **Image Adjustments** dialog. The gallery offers a one-stop shop for applying your adjustments all supported by a dynamic preview window!

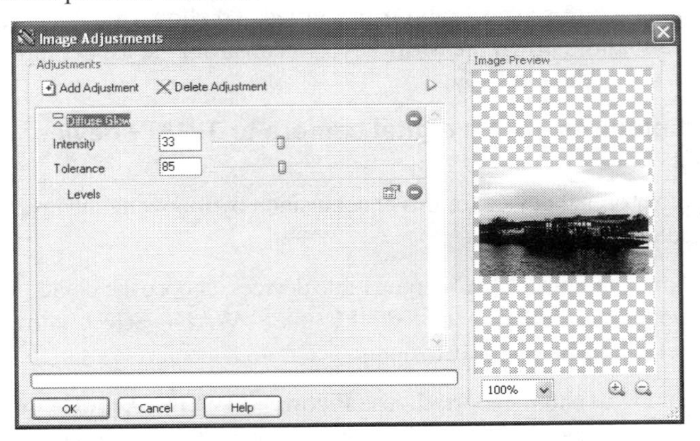

Adjustments and effects can be applied to imported pictures as well as objects converted to pictures within DrawPlus.

Adding an adjustment is as easy as choosing one from the **Add Adjustments** drop-down menu in the Image Adjustments dialog. To assist in the selection of an appropriate adjustment the list is separated into corrective adjustments (in the first half of the list), and effect-inducing adjustments (in the second half).

As soon as an adjustment is selected it is added to a stack where additional adjustments can be added and built up cumulatively. Any adjustment can be switched on/off, deleted or reordered in this list. The order in which they appear in the stack may produce very different results—if you're not happy with your current order—DrawPlus lets you drag and drop your adjustment into any position in the stack.

Adjustments are applied such that the most recently added adjustment always appears at the bottom of the list and is applied to the picture last (after the other adjustments above it). In the above example, the Diffuse Glow effect is applied to the picture first, followed by Levels.

To add an image adjustment:

1. Select the picture that you want to apply an adjustment to.
2. Click the Image Adjustments button on the Picture context toolbar.
3. In the Image Adjustments dialog, click **Add Adjustment**.
4. From the drop-down menu, select an adjustment.
5. There are three methods to configure properties depending on the adjustment selected:

   • Adjust settings by moving available sliders (if present).
   OR
   • Enter different values into the input boxes.
   OR
   • For more complex adjustments, make changes in a pop-up dialog.

Some adjustments have no properties and are applied directly as they are selected.

6. Click the **OK** button.

Add more than one adjustment to the picture by repeating the above procedure.

To delete an image adjustment:

- With an adjustment selected, click the Delete Adjustment button.

To switch on/off adjustments:

- In the same way in which a layer's contents can be made visible/invisible, the **Disable** button can be used to temporarily make an adjustment invisible or visible.

To modify adjustments:

The properties of any selected adjustment can be changed in one of two ways:

- Properties will be displayed alongside the adjustment in the stack (in Image Adjustments dialog)—you can alter and experiment with these.
- The properties of an applied effect or adjustment can be changed by clicking the **Properties** button alongside the effect (in the Image Adjustments dialog). This is because some effects are more complex to modify by their nature and require to be presented in a separate dialog.

To reorder adjustments:

- Adjustments can be moved around the stack to change the order in which they are applied to the picture. Drag an adjustment entry to another position in the list. A dark line indicates the new position in which the entry will be place if the mouse button is released.

Tutorial Resources

For more experience with the tools and techniques covered in this chapter, we recommend these PDF-based tutorials (go to **Help>Tutorials** in DrawPlus):

Try this tutorial...	For practice with these tools and techniques...
Create Filter Effects/ Draw a Flow Chart	Drawing QuickShapes
Create an 8-Ball	Modifying QuickShapes
Draw a Flow Chart	Drawing Connectors
Create a Glass Effect	Drawing Free Text Objects
Create Metallic Text	Using fonts
Work with Line Tools	Importing pictures

Jump between your PDF tutorials and DrawPlus with **Alt-Tab**.

7

Fill, Lines, and Transparency

Introduction

We've seen how to create and manipulate all the basic types of objects—lines, shapes, QuickShapes, and text. It's time now to examine how you can use the Colour, Swatches, Line, and Transparency tabs to apply a remarkable variety of effects to those objects.

Colours, of course, are fundamental to fill and line effects, so we'll also provide details on how to manipulate colours in DrawPlus.

Types of Fills

Any closed shape, such as a closed curve or QuickShape, or text has an interior region that can be filled. The fill type can be **solid**, **gradient**, **bitmap** or **plasma**. Those that use a single colour are solid fills. Let's take a moment to run through them, using a plain old square as an example object.

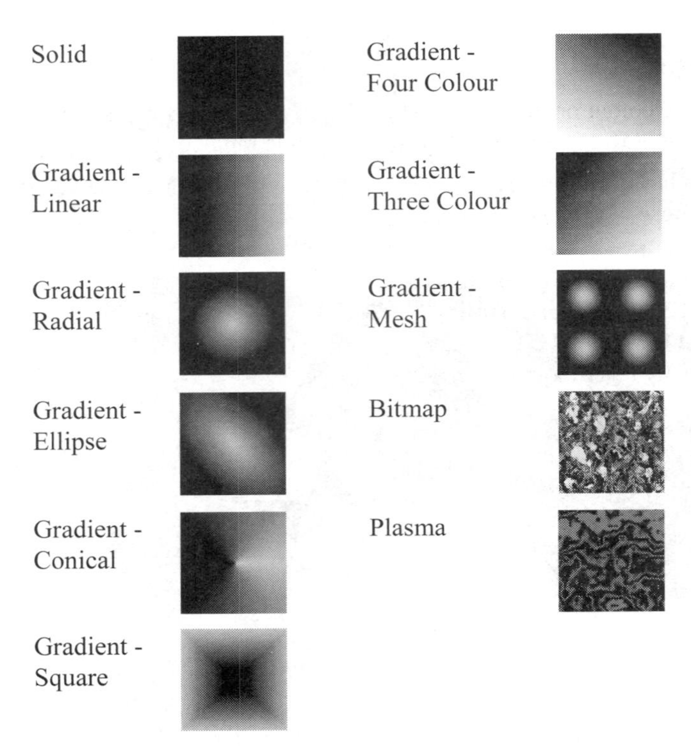

In the above examples, we've used black and white to show the contrast on the different fill types. In DrawPlus, fills can use an unlimited combination of colours from a number of colour models. The Swatches tab displays swatches for all fill types which accurately represents the fill that can be applied. Navigate around the Swatches tab and select as appropriate!

Bitmapand **Plasma** fills apply bitmapped images or patterns to the object, each with unique properties. Think of Bitmap fills as named "pictures" that fill shapes. Plasma (or "fractal") fills use randomised patterns, useful for simulating cloud or shadow effects. **Mesh** fills are especially complex and are covered in more detail on p. 135.

Solid Colours

Applying a line colour or fill is easy, whether you're selecting a custom colour from the **Colour tab** or a preset colour from a whole range of colour swatches in the **Swatches tab**.

The **Colour** tab can operate in several modes available from a drop-down menu—**HSL Wheel** (shown), **HSL Square**, **RGB Sliders**, **CMYK Sliders** and **Tinting**. We'll concentrate on the HSL Wheel which is very popular amongst drawing professionals.

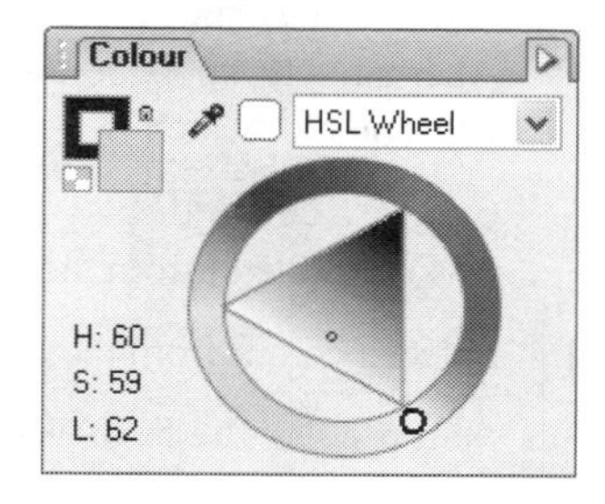

The HSL Wheel is made up of three key components—the line/fill swatches, the outer Hue wheel and the Saturation/Lightness triangle.

The Line/Fill swatches govern whether the selected colour is applied as a line colour, solid fill, or both simultaneously.

The small circles shown in the wheel and triangle indicate the current setting for hue and saturation/lightness, respectively. Drag either circle around to adjust the overall HSL value.

A **Tinting** option in the Colour tab's drop-down menu (not shown above) allows a percentage of shade/tint to be applied to your colour.

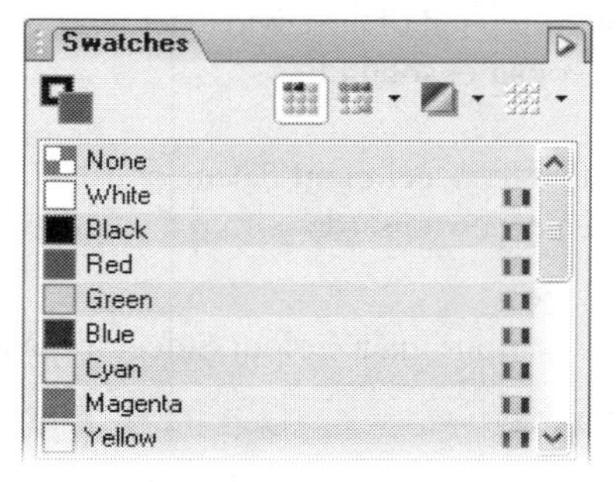

By comparison, the **Swatches** tab hosts a vast array of colour swatches for solid colour, gradient, plasma and bitmap fills.

To apply a custom solid colour via the Colour tab:

1. Select the object(s) and display the Studio's **Colour** tab.
2. Click either the **Line** or **Fill** swatch at the top left of the tab to determine whether the colour is applied as a line colour or solid fill. The swatch which sits in front of the other swatch is considered to be currently active. Alternatively, apply colour to both line and fill simultaneously by clicking **Link** on the swatch.
3. Choose a colour display mode (HSL Wheel, HSL Square, RGB Sliders, or CMYK Sliders) from the drop-down menu.
4. Select a colour from the display.

For example, for the HSL Wheel mode, try the following:

1. Drag the dark circle situated on the outer Hue wheel around the wheel until your chosen hue appears in the Fill swatch.
2. Click in the triangle to set the Saturation and Lightness associated with the previously set hue. The small circle can be moved in any direction.

Exact colour values can be set by double-clicking the Fill or Line swatch.

To apply a solid colour via the Swatches tab:

1. Select the object(s) and display the Studio's **Swatches** tab.
2. Click either the **Line** or **Fill** swatch at the top left of the tab to determine whether the colour is applied as a line colour or solid fill.
3. Pick a thumbnail from either the **Document** Palette or from another palette shown in the **Palettes** drop-down list (drag from the thumbnail onto the object as an alternative).

Alternatively, use **Format>Fill...** to apply colour via a Colour Selector dialog.

To change a fill's shade/tint (lightness):

1. Select the object and set the Fill Swatch in the Colour tab accordingly.
2. From the Colour tab's drop-down menu, select **Tinting**.
3. Drag the **Shade/Tint** slider to the left or right to darken or lighten your starting colour, respectively (the original colour is set at 0%). You can also enter a percentage value in the box (entering 0 or dragging the pointer back to its original position reverts to the original colour).

A tint can be applied to a new colour which can then be saved in your Document Palette (Swatches tab) for future use.

Notes

- To load a different palette, use the **Palettes** drop-down menu in the Swatches tab. For more details, see Managing Colours and Palettes on p. 140.
- Set a transparent interior for objects by using the:
  - Colour tab: select the **No Fill** swatch to apply transparency to an object's line or fill. Ensure the Line/Fill Swatch is set correctly.

OR

  - Swatches tab: Choose the first swatch, **None,** from the preset swatches to apply.

When setting no fill, the Saturation/Lightness triangle disappears on the Colour tab's HSL Wheel as colour is no longer set.

Linked Colours

A **linked colour** is a colour you define as a shade/tint of any existing solid colour (the "**base colour**") created in the Studio's Swatches tab. You can use linked colours just like regular solid colours to fill objects throughout your drawing. Since the colours are linked back to the base colour, if you want to update all linked colours, you simply modify the base colour. When you're creating a complex drawing with numerous shades, for example an illustration of a car with subtle surface curvature and modelling, linked colours can be a real time-saver if you need to change the overall colour from red to blue. Typically, you'll firstly create a base colour (with a unique name of your choosing), then create linked colours as shades of that base colour.

To create a linked base colour:

1. In any palette on the Studio's Swatches tab, right-click and choose **Add Linked....**
   OR
   In the Colour tab, select the **Options** button and choose **Add to Palette (Linked)**.

2. In the Colour Selector dialog, select a base colour from the window (i.e., the colour that all object colours will link to). A thumbnail will appear at the end of the palette.

If you're working with already drawn objects, save your object's fill as a linked base colour by right-clicking and choosing **Format >Fill**. The dialog's Options button let's you **Add to Palette (Linked)**.

Notice that the thumbnails of a linked base colour and a standard solid colour differ—the former displays a small tab in its bottom-right corner. Linked colour presets are also named as Linked Red, Linked Green, etc.

To create object's linked colours:

1. Apply a linked base colour to a specific or multiple object's fill, line or text.
2. In the Colour tab, display the **Tinting** option in the drop-down menu.
3. Select objects one by one, each time applying a different percentage shade/tint drag the **Shade/Tint** slider to change the shading.

Instead of your objects being filled independently a linkage now exists to the same base colour. A simple update of the base colour updates all objects automatically.

The **Tinting** option shows the base colour from which an object's colour is derived.

To update linked colours:

1. In the Swatches tab, right-click the base colour's thumbnail and choose **Edit...**.
2. Use the Colour Selector dialog to define a new colour value.
3. Click **OK**. The gallery thumbnail, and any drawn objects using the linked colours, are updated immediately.

Use **Format Painter** on the Standard toolbar to apply linked colours between objects on the page.

Gradient/bitmap Fills

Gradient fills provide a gradation or spectrum of colours spreading between two or more colours. A gradient fill has an editable path with nodes that mark the origin of each of these key colours. A Bitmap fill uses a named bitmap—often a material, pattern, or background image—to fill a line or object.

DrawPlus supplies preset gradient or Bitmap fills on the Swatches tab, and you can import your own. Both types of fill are arranged into categories within the Swatches tab to make your choice of fill simple and quick.

Applying different transparency effects (using the **Transparency** tab) won't alter the object's fill settings as such, but may significantly alter a fill's actual appearance.

Applying a gradient or Bitmap fill

There are several ways to apply a gradient or Bitmap fill as a line colour or object fill: using the **Fill Tool** or via the **Swatches** tab. Using the Fill Tool, you can vary the fill's path on an object for different effects.

To apply a gradient fill (Fill Tool):

1. Select a coloured object.
2. Click the **Fill Tool** button on the Drawing toolbar.
3. Click and drag on the object to define the fill path (a dashed line). The object takes a simple Linear fill, grading from black to the colour that the object was previously filled with.

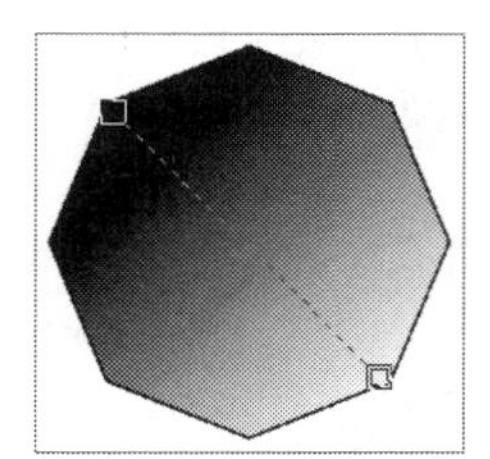

Working with the fill path leads to endless possibilities for editing your gradient fill. See DrawPlus help for more details.

To apply a gradient or Bitmap fill (Swatches tab):

1. Select an object.
2. Click the Swatches tab and ensure the **Fill** swatch is placed in front of **Line** swatch.
3. For gradient fills, select the **Gradient** button's drop-down menu and pick a gradient categories.

   OR

   For bitmap fills, select the **Bitmap** button's drop-down menu and pick a bitmap categories.
4. Click the thumbnail for the fill you want to apply.
   OR
   Drag from the gallery swatch onto any object.

Adjusting an object's fill colours

Editing Solid Fills

Solid fills use a single colour—that is, a specific mixture of components which belong to a specific colour model, e.g.

- HSL: containing Hue, Saturation and Lightness.
- RGB: containing Red, Green and Blue.
- CMYK: Cyan, Magenta, Yellow and Black.

Other types of fills such as gradient fills use at least two. One way of altering a solid colour in a fill after it's been applied to an object is to use the **Colour Selector** dialog.

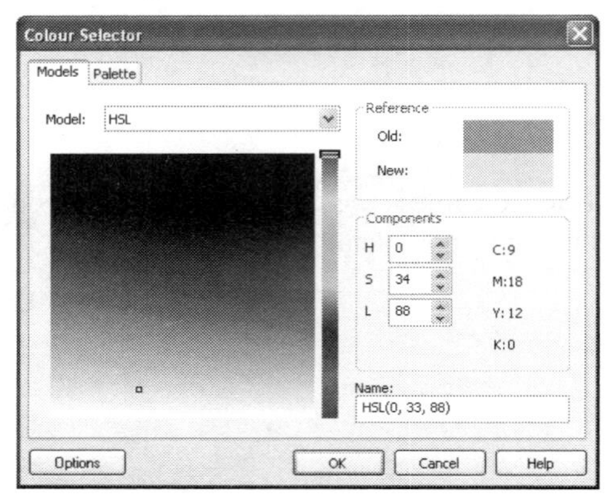

Since the solid fill uses only one colour, the dialog can be used to edit the fill easily by specifying the fill's colour value.

To set a different solid fill:

1. Right-click the object and choose **Format>Fill...** (also available on the Format menu).
2. Use the vertical slider to the immediate right of the colour space window to set your colour value (or use the Input box).
3. Click anywhere in the colour space window then drag the marker around to fine-tune your colour selection.

> You can choose a different **colour model** (such as RGB or CMYK) from the **Model** drop-down menu at any time.

To edit a gradient fill:

1. Select an object with a gradient fill.
2. Choose the **Fill Tool** from the Drawing toolbar. You'll see the object's gradient fill path displayed as a dashed line with a node at either end.
3. Use the cursor to hover over and then drag each node in various directions, while increasing or decreasing the length of the fill path. As you do so, the fill changes position across the object.

Each gradient fill type has a characteristic path. For example, Radial fills have single-line paths, with the gradient initially starting at the object's centre. Ellipse fills likewise begin at the centre, but their paths have two lines so you can adjust the fill's extent in two directions away from the centre. Radial fills are always evenly circular, while Ellipse fills can be skewed in one direction or another.

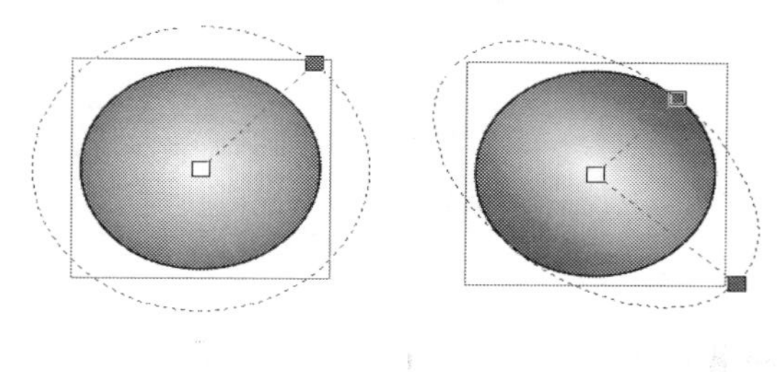

Radial Fill **Ellipse Fill**

You can widen or narrow the gradient's extent, even drag either node completely outside the object. Or, for a Radial fill on a round shape, try placing the start node near the figure's upper edge, off-centre, to create a reflection highlight.

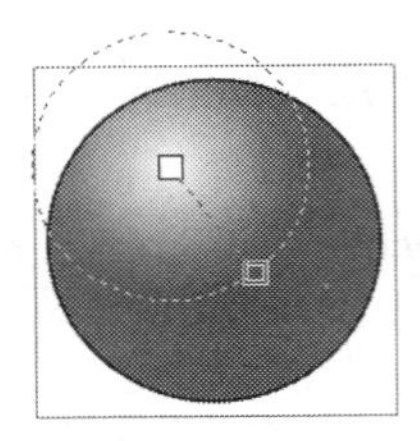

Editing a gradient fill spectrum

Whether you're editing a gradient fill that's been already been applied to an object, or redefining one of the gallery fills, the basic concepts are the same. Whereas solid fills use a single colour, all gradient fills utilize at least two **key colours**, with a spread of hues in between each key colour, creating a "spectrum" effect. You can either edit the fill spectrum directly, using the Fill Tool (where colours can be dragged onto the fill path) or use **Format>Fill** to access the **Gradient Fill Editor** dialog.

The editing of gradient fills is a complex operation and is covered in greater detail in the DrawPlus Help.

Editing Bitmap and Plasma Fills

On Bitmap and Plasma fills, you'll see the fill path displayed as two lines joined at a centre point. Nodes mark the fill's centre and edges. To reposition the fill's centre, drag the centre node. To create a skewed or tilted fill region, drag one or both edge nodes sideways.

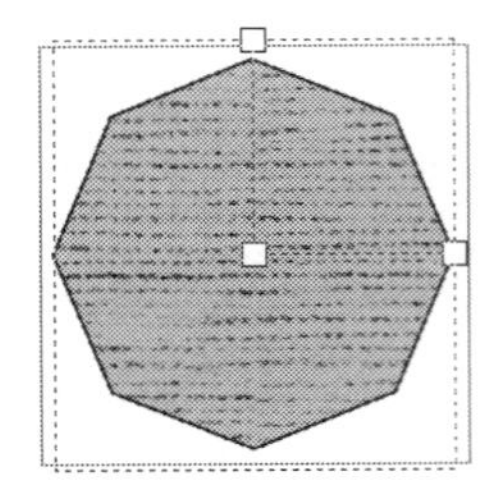

Unlike the other fill types, Bitmap and Plasma fills don't simply "end" at the edges of their fill paths. Rather, they **tile** (repeat) so you can fill indefinitely large regions at any scale. By dragging the edge nodes in or out with the Fill Tool, you can "zoom" in or out on the fill pattern.

Certain settings for Plasma fills are only available via the fill dialog. **Grain** controls the flow of the pattern, with lower values yielding a smoothly flowing ("cloudy") pattern, and higher values displaying more image grain. **Seed** is a random number where each value entered produces a different pattern. Use a larger value for **Size** for better appearance if the fill is being applied to a larger object. If the fill pattern is being tiled (repeated) within the object, check **Tile Inverted** if you want the patterns to flip alternately so tops will touch tops where two fills meet, lefts will touch lefts, and so on.

Working with Mesh Fills

A **Mesh fill** works like a gradient fill but uses a more complex fill path, with a grid or "mesh" of many nodes representing separate key colours. The overall effect, especially useful for multifaceted highlighting, arises from the colour gradients that spread between each of these nodes.

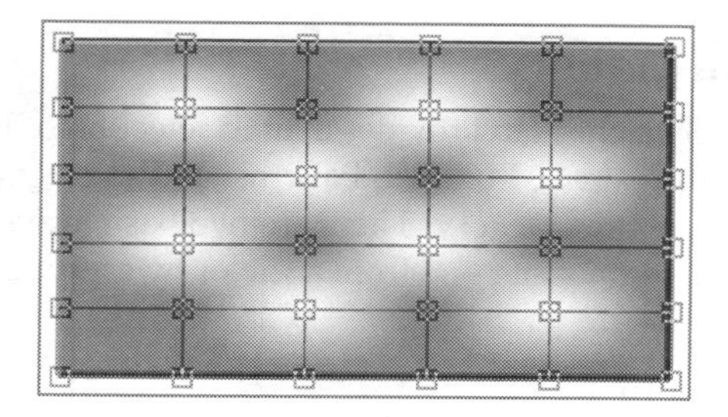

Once you've applied a Mesh fill to an object, you can edit the mesh itself with the Mesh Fill context toolbar to achieve unique results.

To edit a Mesh fill:

1. Select the object possessing a Mesh fill.
2. Choose the **Fill Tool**. The fill's nodes (each representing a key colour) are interconnected by a grid of path lines. The Mesh Fill context toolbar appears.
3. Zoom in so that you can see the individual nodes more clearly. In a Mesh fill, there's a unique gradient along each path connecting two nodes.
4. Click any node with the cursor to select it.
5. Drag the node slightly—for outer nodes the object shape will be altered, while moving an inner node will alter the original distribution of that selected node's key colour.

6. To change the node to a different key colour, select the node and pick a solid colour from the Colour tab or Swatches tab. Alternatively, drag a solid colour thumbnail from any palette in the Swatches tab directly over the selected node until a plus cursor appears. Release the mouse button.

You can select multiple nodes by **Shift-**clicking them in turn, or dragging a marquee around them.

Looking closely, **control handles** appear on any selected node and adjacent nodes. The number of handles per node will vary, depending on the number of adjacent nodes. Mesh fill path lines and nodes behave very much like intersecting curves and curve nodes, and can be adjusted as described in Editing Curves on p. 73. Simple warping effects, colour spread changes and and path line curvature can all be affected. Nodes can be added and deleted at any time.

Using the Bitmap Fill Gallery

The Bitmap gallery on the Swatches tab provides a large selection of bitmaps, grouped into categories like Abstract, Material, Patterns, and so on. You can add or delete a bitmap or an entire category. There are two basic ways to add Bitmap fills to the gallery: by importing one from a file or by creating one in DrawPlus.

To add an imported bitmap:

1. Select the **Bitmap** button in the Swatches tab and choose the **My Bitmaps** category (or any created category).
2. Right-click anywhere in the gallery and choose **Add...**.
3. From the dialog, navigate to and select your new bitmap to import.
4. Select **Open**. The new fill swatch is added to the gallery.

The bitmap could also have been converted from a drawn vector object with **Tools>Convert to Bitmap...**. Bitmaps which currently exist on the page can be added to any gallery.

To add a created bitmap (from an object):

1. Select the bitmap converted from your drawing object.
2. Ensure the correct Bitmap gallery is displayed—this is where your fill will be placed!
3. Right-click the bitmap and choose **Add to Studio>Fill**.
4. In the dialog, enter a file name and pick the file location (DrawPlus needs to store the bitmap as a separate file).
5. Select **Save**.

Both methods will result in your new bitmap appearing in your chosen gallery ready for future use.

To delete a Bitmap fill from the gallery:

- Right-click the thumbnail and choose **Delete**. Click **Yes** to confirm deletion. You can optionally choose to delete the bitmap file from your computer permanently.

Deleting a gallery fill doesn't affect any objects that have already been given that fill.

To add a category to the Bitmap fill gallery:

1. Display the **Swatches** tab.
2. With the **Bitmap** button selected, click on the **Options** button and select **Add Category...** from the sub-menu.
3. Type a category name into the dialog, and click **OK**. A new empty gallery category is added to the category list and is displayed immediately for you to add new bitmap fills to.

To delete a category from the Bitmap fill gallery:

1. Display the **Swatches** tab.
2. Use the **Bitmap** button to select the category to be deleted. Click on the **Options** button and select **Delete Category** from the menu. You are asked to confirm deletion.

Setting the default fill

See Using Object Defaults on p. 60.

Defining Colours and Palettes

When you're applying a **solid fill** or **line colour** using the Studio's Swatches tab, you choose a colour from one of several colour **palettes**, arranged as colour swatches. Different palettes can be loaded but only one palette is displayed at any one time. Several of the colour palettes are based on "themed" colours while the remaining palettes are based on industry-standard colour models, i.e.

- **RGB**: Red, Green and Blue (default)
- **CMYK**: Cyan, Magenta, Yellow and Black

Palettes can be loaded, created, deleted and saved as discussed in Managing Colours and Palettes on p. 140.

Changing the Set of Gallery Colours

Colours are added manually or automatically from the **Colour tab** or taken directly from a drawing object's line/fill into the user's **Document Palette**. The palette also stores commonly used colours (e.g., Red, Green, Blue, etc.). Once a colour is stored in the Document Palette, it can be edited with the Colour Selector dialog at any time. Colours can also be added, deleted, or renamed within the Document Palette as in any of the other Swatches tab's palettes.

To add a new colour to the Document Palette:

1. Either:
   - Select a colour mixed from the Colour tab.

   OR

   1. Use the **Colour Picker** on the Colour tab to select any colour already on your page. Click on the dropper icon (hold down the mouse button for magnification) and select your chosen pickup colour with the pickup cursor. The colour is picked up in the **Picked Colour** swatch.
   2. Click this swatch to transfer the colour to the **Fill** swatch.
2. Click the **Options** button on the Colour tab.
3. If **Automatically Add to Document Palette** is checked, the colour will have been added immediately—if unchecked, click **Add to palette** to add it manually.

If the colour doesn't already exist in the Swatches tab's Document Palette, a new thumbnail appears for it.

To add a new colour from the Swatches tab:

1. Display the **Document Palette** from the Swatches tab.
2. Right-click any solid colour thumbnail and choose **Add...**.
3. From the Colour Selector dialog, click on a new position in the colour space window to set a new colour. Alternatively, enter values in the adjacent input boxes.
4. Click **OK**. Scroll to the bottom of the gallery to see your new thumbnail.

To add an object's fill to the Document Palette:

1. Select the object and set the Swatches tab's Fill swatch.
2. Right-click the object and choose **Add to Studio>Fill...** (or choose from the Format menu). A new thumbnail appears at the bottom of the Document Palette.

You can also change the definition of any preset colour or fill that appears in the Swatches tab. The process is comparable to adjusting an object's "local" fill, but your change will be permanently available as an updated gallery thumbnail for future use.

To edit any solid colour fill:

1. Right-click a sample in any solid colour palette of the Swatches tab and choose **Edit...**.
2. Choose a different colour from the colour spectrum in the **Colour Selector** dialog.
3. Click the **OK** button. The colour and its thumbnail are permanently updated.

In passing, notice that right-clicking on a thumbnail also provides the option of deleting its colour or fill. Keep in mind that there's no Undo for this action, so you may want to reserve it for managing your own custom fills (or if there's a preset you really don't care for!).

To remove a colour:

- Right-click on the colour in any palette of the Swatches tab and choose **Delete**.

Managing Colours and Palettes

DrawPlus ships with a varied selection of palettes, stored separately as .PLT files. The RGB and CMYK palettes can be loaded, along with other "themed" palettes including Earth, Pastels, and Soft Tones. The "themed" palettes offer an alternative to using the RGB and CMYK palettes. Palettes can also be created, deleted and, for the Document Palette, saved.

Colours in the Document Palette are just saved locally, so they don't automatically carry over to new documents. However changes to the other palettes are saved globally, in that colour changes will carry over to new documents automatically.

To load a named palette:

1. In the Swatches tab, click the down arrow on the **Palettes** button.
2. From the resulting drop-down menu, select the Standard, CMYK, RGB or "themed" palette, or a palette that you've created yourself.

The loaded palette's colours appear as swatches in the **Swatches** tab, replacing the swatches previously visible.

To create a new custom palette:

1. With the **Palettes** button selected in the Swatches tab, click the **Options** button in the top right-hand corner and choose **Add New Palette...**.
2. Enter a name for the new palette and click **OK**. The new empty palette is displayed and its name will appear in the Palettes drop-down menu.

To delete a new custom palette:

1. In the Swatches tab, select the palette for deletion from **Palettes** button's drop-down list.
2. Click the **Options** button in the top right-hand corner and choose **Delete Palette**.... After confirmation, the palette is removed from the list.

To save the Document Palette:

1. Right-click on any colour thumbnail in the Document Palette and choose **Palette Manager**.
2. In the dialog, choose the **Options** button pick **Save Palette As...** and save the palette to a new .PLT file.

If you store the file in another folder to the initially prompted one, then your saved palette will not appear in the **Palettes** drop-down menu.

Using the Colour Selector

The Colour Selector is a complementary dialog to the Colour and Swatches tabs and is accessible from **Format>Fill**. It lets you choose a colour to apply from a range of different palettes and allows you to mix custom colours.

- The **Models** tab displays the colour space of several established colour models: RGB (red, green blue), HSL (hue, saturation, lightness), CMYK (cyan, magenta, yellow, black), and PANTONE colours.
- The **Palette** tab displays the colours currently present in the Swatches tab's Document Palette, i.e. your drawing's current palette. The Document Palette can be saved as described above.

To add a PANTONE® colour to the Document Palette:

- Select **Format>Fill** to display the Colour Selector dialog, then in the Model list on the **Models** tab choose **PANTONE Colors**.
- Select a PANTONE colour from one of the libraries listed in the **Palette** list. These include PANTONE Color Bridge libraries for European and US print standards.
- Choose the **Add to Palette** button to add the colour to the Document Palette.

For more details about **PANTONE®** colours see Colour Matching with PANTONE® or Serif Colours on p. 152.

Lines

Chapter 4 introduced us to drawing lines—both straight and curved. Previously in this chapter we looked at how to apply solid colours and even gradient/bitmap fills to the line itself. We'll now focus on effects that can be applied to plain lines!

Remember that as well as freeform, straight, or curved lines most DrawPlus objects, including closed shapes, free text objects, and QuickShapes, possess **line properties** such as colour, weight, scaling, style, and termination (start and end).

Line properties are modified in the **Line** tab. You can adjust line width, and line styles for the line ends and body.

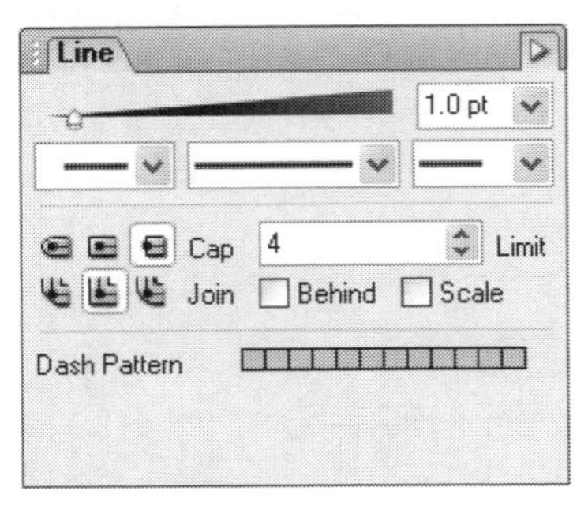

Chain lines (also known as picture tubes) are a type of line which repeat bitmaps along the length of a line to create unusual picture-based patterns. These are controlled via the **Line Styles** tab and are described further in Chain Lines on p. 194.

Applying line properties

To change line properties of a selected object:

- Use the Swatches tab to change the line's colour and/or shade. (If changing the outline colour of a shape or other object, click the **Line** swatch so it displays in front of the **Fill** swatch). Click a gallery sample from the Swatches tab's Solid, Gradient or Bitmap galleries to apply that colour or fill to the selected object's line. Alternatively, use the Colour tab to apply a colour to the line from a colour mixer.

- Use the **Line** tab to change the line's weight (thickness), type, or other properties. Select a line width with the slider, and use the drop-down boxes to pick the type of line.

The middle **Line Styles** drop-down menu provides **Single**, **Calligraphic**, and several **Dashed** and **Double** styles. Each produces the following styles:

Calligraphic and Dashed line styles can be further customized, i.e.

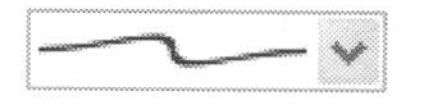

For Calligraphic lines of variable width (drawn as if with a square-tipped pen held at a certain angle), use the **Calligraphy Angle** box to set the angle of the pen tip, i.e.

For Dashed lines, drag the Dash Pattern slider to set the overall pattern length (the number of boxes to the left of the slider) and the dash length (the number of those boxes that are black). The illustrations below show lines with pattern and dash lengths of (**1**) 4 and 2, and (**2**) 5 and 4:

Select the "Double line" presets from the menu to see how they are structured.

The Line tab also lets you vary a line's **Cap** (end) and the **Join** (corner) where two lines intersect. Both properties tend to be more conspicuous on thicker lines; joins are more apparent with more acute angles. The respective button icons clearly communicate each setting:

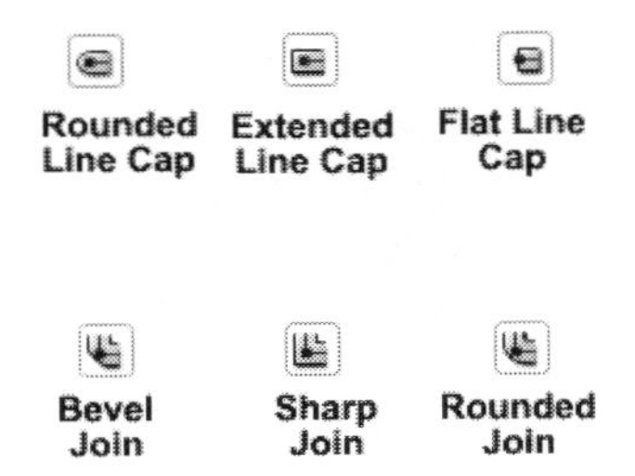

The **Behind** option controls line width relative to object size—useful with very small objects or when resizing text. When checked, the object's line appears behind its fill; otherwise, the fill is drawn in front of the line.

Check the **Scale** button to automatically expand and contract the line thickness in proportion to the object size or uncheck to make the line's thickness remain unchanged. When scaling text, for example, you might either want the border to remain the same width, or change in proportion to the overall characters.

Adding new plain line styles

If you've customized a plain line's attributes as described above, you can add its line style to the Line Style tab's "Plain" gallery so that it will be available to use again. You can also delete any existing gallery style.

To add a plain line's style to the Line Styles tab:

1. Display the Line Styles tab's "Plain" category. Note that the tab is switched off by default.
2. Select an object with line attributes and click the Line Style tab's **Add Line to Gallery** button.

A thumbnail depicting the new line style appears at the bottom of the "Plain" gallery.

To delete a plain line style:

- Right-click its thumbnail and choose **Delete Line**.

Deleting a line style doesn't affect any objects that already use the line.

Adjusting an object's line tint and colour

For any standalone or object's line, you can adjust its tint (lightness) and colour, just as you can for the object fill. Ensure the Line swatch is active in the Colour or Swatches tab. See p. 128 for more information on applying tinting.

Setting the default line

See Using Object Defaults on p. 60.

Using Format Painter

The **Format Painter** is used to copy one object's line and fill properties directly to another object, including between line/shape and text objects.

1. Select the object that has the properties you want to copy.
2. Click the **Format Painter** button on the Standard toolbar. When you click the button, the selected object's formatting is "picked up." The cursor changes to a paintbrush and the next object you click takes on the original object's properties.

To cancel Format Painter mode, click on a blank area, or choose any tool button.

For copy formatting from one text object to another, a number of other text properties (font, style, and so on) besides line and fill are passed along at the same time.

Transparency

Transparency effects are great for highlights, shading and shadows, and simulating "rendered" realism. They can make the critical difference between flat-looking illustrations and those with depth and snap.

Understanding transparency may seem a bit tricky because by definition, you can't "see" it the way you can see a colour fill applied to an object. In fact, it's there all the time in DrawPlus. Each new object has a transparency property: the default just happens to be "None"—that is, no transparency (opaque).

Let's check out the Transparency tab. As with the Swatches tab, there are galleries for solid, gradient and bitmap transparencies.

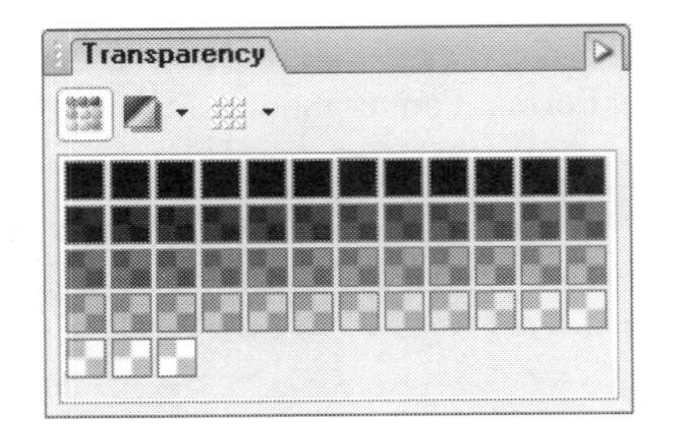

Each preset's tooltip is expressed in percentage Opacity, an attribute of the Transparency effect. Think of this as the inverse of transparency—0% Opacity = 100% Transparency and vice versa.

Transparency: The “vanishing” fill

Transparencies work rather like fills that use “disappearing ink” instead of colour. The more transparency in a particular spot, the more “disappearing” takes place there, and the more the object(s) underneath show through. Just as a gradient fill can vary from light to dark, a transparency can vary from more to less, i.e. from clear to opaque, as in the illustration:

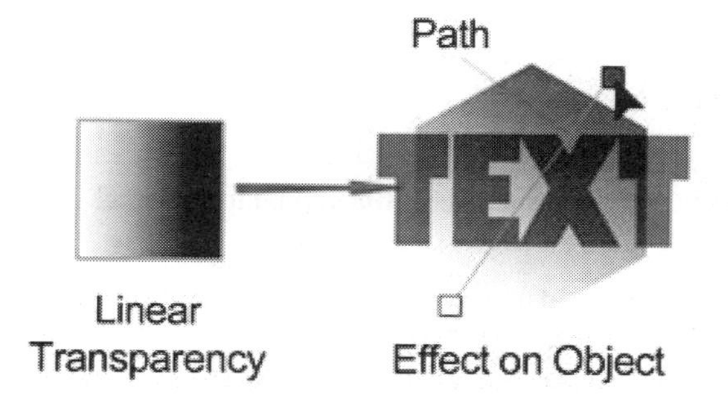

Here, the hexagonal shape has had a Linear transparency applied, with more transparency at the lower end of the path and less at the upper end.

In DrawPlus, transparency effects work very much like greyscale fills, in that they can be applied along an editable path, and they can be applied as a custom transparency or from a range of preset thumbnails. Another similarity is that all transparency effect names are comparable to the fills of the same name, i.e. solid, gradient and bitmap transparencies are available.

- **Solid** transparency distributes the transparency evenly across the object.
- **Gradient** transparencies (Linear, Radial, Ellipse, Conical, Plasma, Square, Four Colour, Three Colour) provide a range of simple to complex gradient effects, which range from clear to opaque.
- **Bitmap** transparencies host texture maps under a series of categories. (To review the concept, see Gradient/bitmap Fills on p. 131)

Applying transparency

There are two ways to apply transparency: via the **Transparency** tab or by using the **Transparency Tool**.

For gradient transparency, you can adjust the transparency effect by adding or subtracting nodes from the gradient transparency path— this changes the degree of transparency along the path and the extent to which the transparency changes (see Adjusting an object’s gradient transparency on p. 149).

To apply transparency with Transparency tab:

1. With your object selected, go to the **Transparency** tab.
2. For solid transparency, select the **Solid** button and pick a thumbnail from the gallery. The lighter portions of the samples represent more transparency (expressed as percentage Opacity).
   OR:
   For gradient transparency, choose the **Gradient** button and pick your thumbnail from a range of categories.
   OR:
   For Bitmap transparency, choose the **Bitmap** button and pick a thumbnail.
3. The transparency effect is applied to the object.

Sometimes objects of a lighter colour will not display their transparency clearly—ensure the transparency is applied correctly by temporarily placing the object over a strong solid colour.

To apply gradient transparency with Transparency Tool:

1. Select an object.
2. Click the **Transparency Tool** button on the Drawing toolbar.
3. Click and drag on the object to define the transparency path. The object takes a simple Linear transparency, grading from 100% to 0% opacity.

Adjusting an object's solid transparency

For objects with solid transparency, the level of transparency can be adjusted with the Transparency tab by simply clicking a different transparency preset.

Adjusting an object's gradient transparency

You'll recall that different fill types have different paths. The same concept applies to transparency effects, which can be edited with the Transparency Tool rather than the Fill Tool.

For objects with Gradient transparencies (Linear, Radial, Ellipse, etc.) all possess transparency paths, which closely resemble those of their fill counterparts. The Transparency Tool can display an object's gradient transparency, indicated by two or more nodes situated along a path. You can reposition the nodes to adjust the transparency's starting point or end point, or if more than two nodes are present, intermediate levels of transparency along the path.

For transparencies with multiple nodes, each node has its own value, comparable to a key colour in a gradient fill. Each node value can be altered directly on the page, by using the Gradient Transparency Editor dialog or the Transparency tab. The dialog offers more precise control over more complex gradient transparencies.

At the top, the dialog displays the transparency gradient, with pointers marking the nodes (corresponding to nodes on the path) that define specific transparency values. Again, black represents 100% opacity, and white represents 0% opacity, with greyscale values in between. A sample window at the lower right shows the overall transparency effect.

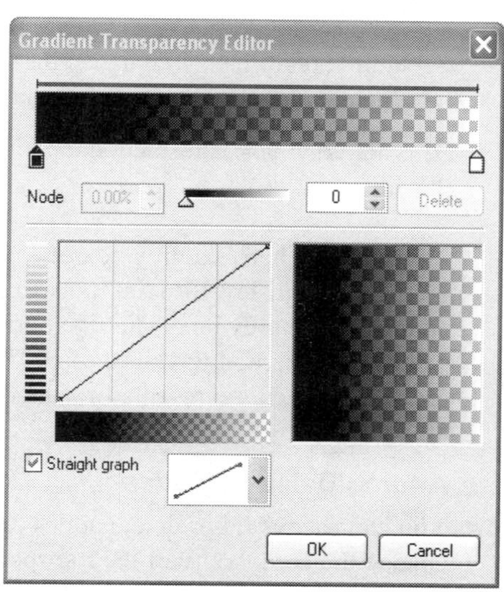

Using the editor is exactly like working with gradient fills, as covered earlier in the chapter. You can add, move, or delete nodes, change their value, and use the contour line to adjust the spread of values between pairs of nodes.

To edit a node's transparency on the page:

1. Right-click an object with a gradient transparency and choose **Format>Transparency** (or choose the command from the Format menu).
2. In the Gradient Transparency Editor dialog, select the node pointer under the transparency gradient window so that the node is selected (not).
3. Drag the **Level** slider (right toward opaque, left toward clear) or type a specific percentage into the **Value** box for the node.
4. If required, apply a smoothing effect between nodes from the lower graph drop-down menu (or edit the nodes in the graph itself).

To edit a node's transparency with Transparency tab:

1. Select an object with a gradient transparency.
2. Pick the Transparency Tool from the Drawing toolbar.
3. Select the **Solid** Transparency gallery of the Transparency tab.
4. Drag a sample thumbnail from the gallery directly onto a node on the transparency path. The lighter the sample applied to a node, the less opaque (more transparent) the effect at that point.

Alternatively, you can select the node and click a sample thumbnail to apply the edit.

For example, here's a grey box over a black box, with multi-level Radial transparency applied to the grey box. The five nodes have been set to alternating values of 100% white and 100% black, represented by the thumbnails at the right.

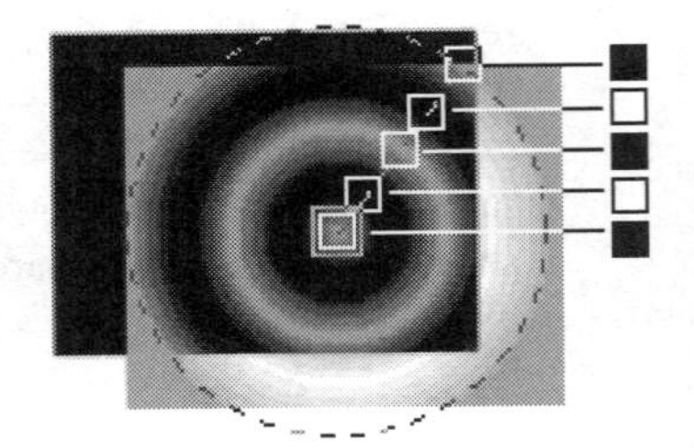

Adding/Deleting Nodes

You can easily add or delete nodes (other than the start and end nodes) to change the complexity of the transparency.

- To add a node, drag from a Transparency tab thumbnail onto a portion of the transparency path where there is no node.
- To delete a node, select it and press **Delete**.

Plasma and Bitmap transparencies

The plasma category available from the **Gradient** button offers plasma transparencies which primarily produce a cloudy effect, while the dedicated **Bitmap** gallery includes **texture maps** based on the Swatches tab's selection of bitmaps. For both transparencies, the path determines the centre and two edges of the effect.

For Plasma transparencies only, you can edit the effect on an object by right-clicking the object and choosing **Format>Transparency**. The **Plasma Transparency Editor** dialog lets you set different **Seed** values to produce different random patterns; **Grain** affects the pattern's flow, and larger **Size** values are better suited to larger objects. The Fill tint sets a percentage tint for the fill while **Tile Inverted** flips the patterns alternately where they tile together. Experiment for the best local effect.

Changing gallery transparencies

If you've defined a new transparency on an object by setting a path and/or level, you can add it to the set of shared gallery transparencies shown on the Transparency tab so that it will be available to use again. You can also edit or delete any of the gallery transparencies.

To add an object's transparency to the gallery:

- Right-click the object and choose **Add to Studio>Transparency...**, or select the same command from the Format menu.

You'll be prompted to give the transparency a name—a new thumbnail will subsequently appear at the bottom of the appropriate gallery in the Transparency tab. Solid transparencies will be added to the Solid transparency gallery, and gradient and bitmap transparencies to the gradient and bitmap galleries.

To edit or delete a gallery transparency, right-click its thumbnail and choose **Edit** or **Delete**.

You cannot edit a bitmap transparency.

Colour Matching with PANTONE® or Serif Colours

When it comes to colour reproduction, printing devices and computer screens are on totally different "wavelengths."

Printing creates colours by mixing inks which absorb light. Mix the four CMYK **process inks** (Cyan, Magenta, Yellow, and blacK), and you get black. No ink gives you white (i.e., the colour of the paper)—so if you want white, you must use no ink! CMYK is a **subtractive** model: the more ink applied, the less light reflected, hence the darker the colour.

A monitor produces an image by mixing light using the three primary colours—Red, Green and Blue—hence, RGB. RGB is an **additive** model. Mix all three colours together and you get white light. Turn all the elements off and you get black. Different brightnesses of each element give the typical computer monitor a range or **gamut** of colours much greater than can be printed with CMYK inks.

The fundamental difference between the CMYK and RGB colour models, and the limited gamut of the printed page compared to the computer screen, create the **colour matching** problem: the challenge of getting your printed output to match what you see in your on-screen drawing layout. By calibrating your equipment and using great care, you can achieve a close approximation—but the cardinal rule is "Trust, but verify!" Never simply assume the colours on your screen will turn out exactly the same when printed. It's just very difficult to convert accurately between the two models!

For accurate colour reproduction, use the Serif *Colour Chart*, available separately. The chart includes swatches of standard CMYK colours printed on two different finishes of paper. Pick the colours you like from the paper swatches and then use only those colours as you design your document. When you've started with a New Drawing, the Swatches tab displays a set of colours identical to those on the Serif Colour Chart—select "CMYK" from the **Palettes** button's drop-down menu to view them. Use these colours and standard CMYK colours for printing, and you're guaranteed a match between the chart samples and your finished piece!

Another solution is to use the PANTONE Colour Selector, built into DrawPlus, which lets you add PANTONE colours to the colour palette. The PANTONE Colour Matching system is an internationally recognized system for colour matching. When a PANTONE colour is output, DrawPlus uses optimized colour values to achieve a better colour match. The on-screen colour display is only an approximation—don't rely on it for accurate colour matching. For precise reproduction, use official PANTONE colour reference materials (swatches).

The International Colour Consortium (ICC) defines industry standards for converting colour information between various colour spaces and gamuts. For more accurate results, we strongly recommend that you take advantage of DrawPlus's colour management features, which let you select ICC device profiles that specify how the internal RGB and/or CMYK colours in your document's fills and bitmaps will map to on-screen and printed colours. Choose **Colour Management...** from the Tools menu to view a dialog that lets you select from profiles available on your system. Your monitor or printer manufacturer's Web site should have additional information on how those devices use ICC profiles. Another good source is **www.color.org**.

A good rule of thumb, if you're especially concerned about colour accuracy, is to produce a Cromalin, Matchprint, or other press proof prior to running the print job. It won't exactly match your final printed page, but will perform a final check that the colours are OK at the prepress stage. Don't authorize the print run until you're happy with your colours as seen in the proof!

Managing Screen and Output Colours

Regardless of the level of colour management you implement, accurate **colour calibration** of your monitor is important. And if you're trying to visually match onscreen colours to a printed page, it's critical. Note that after successful calibration, monitor colours will appear less vibrant as they will be restricted to the gamut of colours that printed inks can achieve.

All computer monitors needs RGB data to display onscreen. However, one monitor's interpretation of RGB green might be different from another's. **Colour profiles** exist to iron out the differences. DrawPlus supports a colour profile called **sRGB**. If you set your monitor to its sRGB mode (check the manufacturer's instructions), you can be assured that DrawPlus is displaying colours as realistically as possible. Some monitors have their own colour profile instead. DrawPlus lets you load a specific monitor's profile (see DrawPlus help), again ensuring accurate colour display. Be sure to choose a colour palette (CMYK or RGB) as described above to match the type of output you're aiming for.

Another approach favoured by professionals is to employ specialized hardware or software to verify that screen colours match established standards. Check the Web for products and advice.

For many non-professionals, a common-sense approach and a few adjustments will help to prevent disastrous mismatches between onscreen and printed work. Here are a few things to keep in mind:

- **Ambient lighting**
  The type and quality of background lighting at your workspace can seriously affect your perception of colours displayed on the monitor. The same monitor display can appear very different under fluorescent lighting, which has a bluish tinge, than under warmer, redder incandescent lighting. Daylight itself is quite variable over the course of a day or even a few moments. Ideally you should work where the light source is consistent (e.g. not a mix of natural and artificial), evenly distributed (no dimmers) and directed downwards to minimize screen reflections. Walls should be a neutral colour. Obviously this is not practical for the average home user but it is something that the small business user should be aware of.

- **Warm-up time**
  The balance of colours displayed on your monitor can vary as it warms up. Allow the monitor to reach a steady temperature before adjusting it.

- **Monitor controls**
  Set the monitor controls to the optimum as recommended in the manufacturer's instructions. Once you have set the controls, tape over them to ensure that they are not accidentally moved (or changed by another user) after calibration.

- **Age**
  The phosphors used in monitors age, causing the colour spectrum to shift over time. This may mean that your monitor output no longer matches the original specification and that the original device profile is no longer appropriate. If the colour balance of your monitor is very important, you should consider replacing it at intervals.

Tutorial Resources

For more experience with the tools and techniques covered in this chapter, we recommend these PDF-based tutorials (go to **Help>Tutorials** in DrawPlus):

Try this tutorial...	For practice with these tools and techniques...
Create3D Effects	Applying solid colour
Work with Line Tools	Transparency tab
Create a Velvet Effect	Fill Tool, Applying Mesh fills. Linked Colours
Create Metallic Effects	Metallic effects, Applying Gradient fills, Plasma fills, Fill Tool, Add Fill to Gallery
Create an 8-Ball	Transparency Tool, Radial Fills
Create a Wine Glass	Transparency Tool, Radial Transparency

Jump between your PDF tutorials and DrawPlus with **Alt-Tab**.

8
Using Layout Tools

Introduction

If you are trying to create a more complex drawing, or an accurate drawing, or a scale drawing, or just a drawing task that you have to repeat on a regular basis—then you need some organization. You need techniques that allow you to position and draw accurately without effort, and tricks that enable you to organize a drawing so that you can work on one part of it without fear of changing another. And you need to set defaults that save you from having to edit every new object.

Toolbars and Tabs

Toolbars and Studio tabs are initially arranged in a convenient layout around the perimeter of the work area. However, you have full control over this arrangement, and can customize the display any way you want—by showing or hiding bars and tabs, docking/undocking or repositioning them onscreen in a way that suits your style.

Toolbars, namely Standard, Drawing, Web, Animation, and View, can be repositioned vertically as well as horizontally, except for the Context and Hintline toolbars.

Customizing toolbars

To show (or hide) a toolbar:

1. Choose **Toolbars** from the View menu.
2. Check (or uncheck) the toolbar name.

OR

- Right-click on any toolbar name, and in the Toolbars flyout check or uncheck the relevant entry as desired.

To reposition a toolbar:

- You may wish to keep the original arrangement of toolbars exactly the same. But if you like, you can reposition the toolbar by clicking and dragging the **gripper bar** at the left or top of the bar.

Toolbars can float anywhere onscreen, or dock (join) with the edges of the DrawPlus window.

To dock a toolbar:

1. Click its gripper bar and drag to the desired location.

2. Drop the item into position when the interface responds.

Customizing Studio tabs

Initially, the tabs appear in several groups at the right edge of the workspace. In this form the groupings behave as single multi-tabbed toolbars, including a **gripper bar** next to the left-most tab in the group. This lets you reposition the whole group.

You can undock individual tabs as floating "tab windows", group them into different group arrangements, and float/dock (as for toolbars) anywhere on the workspace. Any tab or tab group can be collapsed or expanded.

Within a given group of tabs, you can only view one tab's contents at a time. You can pick the arrangement that works best for you—separate tabs that you can view simultaneously, or grouped tabs to conserve screen space.

To minimize space devoted to tabs, two options are available. The **Auto optimize tab size** option in **Tools>Options>Studio** can be used to dynamically resize all tabs to the dimensions of a previously resized tab within the same tab group. Switch off the option to minimize the tab sizes within the same tab group. A second option, **Tabs Collapse Order**, sets the priority for the order in which tabs will automatically collapse when tab space becomes limited.

To collapse/expand tabs:

- To collapse, double-click the tab label of a selected tab (either separate or in a group). To expand, single-click the label.

OR:

1. Click the **Options** button on the right-hand corner of an individual tab's window or the entire tab group.
2. Select **Collapse** or **Expand** from the drop-down menu.

To switch off specific tabs/all tabs in a group:

1. Click the **Options** button at the right-hand corner of the tab group.
2. For specific tabs, uncheck the relevant tab name in the Studio Tab's flyout menu.

OR

- Switch tabs on or off via **View>Studio Tabs**.

To switch on/off all docked tabs:

- Go to **View>Studio Tabs** and check/uncheck the **Hide/Show Studio Tabs** option. Any undocked tabs will remain displayed.

To undock/dock an individual tab:

- To undock, drag the tab's label to its new position (away from the tab group).
- To dock, double-click on the tab's blue top bar (not the tab label).

To undock/dock a tab group:

- Double-click on the tab group's gripper.

To reposition a floating tab on the screen:

- Drag the tab by its tab label to its new position.

To arrange auto collapse of tabs:

1. Display the **Studio** pane in **Tools>Options**.
2. Arrange the tabs in the Tab Collapse Order list with tabs least likely to collapse at the top and those most likely to collapse at the bottom. Use the **Move Up** and **Move Down** buttons to arrange the tab order.

Managing your Workspace

At some point in your session you may want to save the layout of your tabs in the current workspace, with respect to positioning, their size, whether they are switched on/off and if docked or not. This is easy to achieve by selecting **Studio Tabs>Save Workspace...** in the View menu. The settings are saved to a Workspace file (*.wtb) and location of your choice.

At any point you can reset the workspace to its default state by selecting **Studio Tabs>Reset Workspace** or load another previously saved Workspace .wtb file using **Studio Tabs>Load Workspace...**; both options are available via the View menu.

Note that your DrawPlus tool properties and view settings remain unaffected.

Working with Multiple Pages

When you're designing a multi-page document, DrawPlus provides a variety of ways of getting quickly to the place you need to work. The HintLine toolbar at the bottom of the screen provides basic navigation buttons.

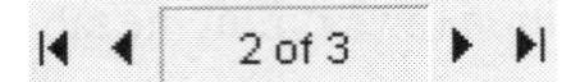

The Current Page box in the centre of the group displays the number of the page(s) you're viewing. Click the buttons to its left to display the **First Page** and **Previous Page**; those to its right for the **Next Page** and **Last Page** of the document.

To add, delete, or copy pages, click the **Add/Delete Pages** button to display the Page Manager.

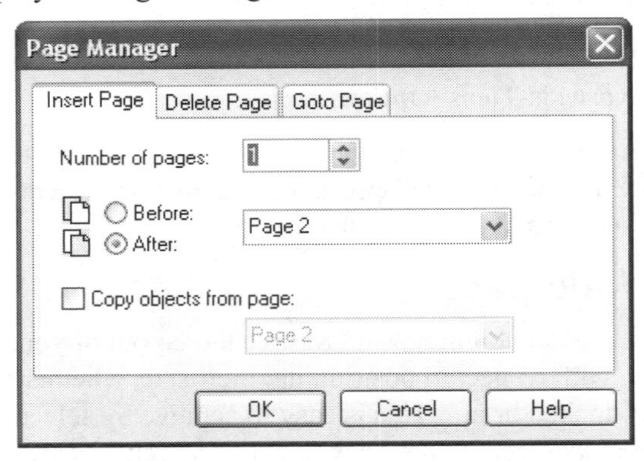

On the Insert Page tab, you can specify how many pages to add, and where to add them. Check **Copy objects from page** if you want to duplicate a particular page. The Delete Page tab provides options for removing pages, and the Goto Page tab affords navigation.

The document format (as determined in **File>Page Setup...**) will determine whether or not you can add or delete pages. For example, Folded documents have a fixed number of pages.

Positioning Aids

DrawPlus provides you with many aids for positioning objects accurately and in relation to one another. Many of them you have been using, perhaps without giving them a thought, from the first time you used DrawPlus.

The main positioning aids are:

- Rulers
- Guides
- Snapping grid

Rulers

The **rulers** that surround the page allow you to measure the exact position of an object. Perhaps because they are so obvious and simple, the rulers tend to be ignored—but if you know how to use them they are a powerful tool.

You can change the units shown on the rulers if necessary (see Measurement Units and Scale on p. 168). The default units are centimetres in Drawing Mode and pixels in Animation Mode. For illustration purposes, we'll assume the rulers are marked in centimetres.

The size of the scale divisions that you actually see depends on the zoom factor you are using. DrawPlus selects sensible units for you and this means that if you need to do accurate work you should zoom in.

When you select an object the rulers not only show its position, but also its extent by a lighter coloured area (also showing the object's dimensions).

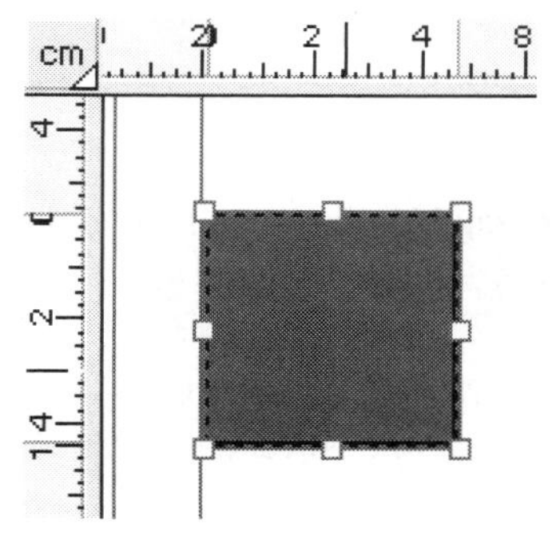

You can even move the rulers away from their default top-left position by dragging the ruler intersection (showing the type of measurement unit) downwards and to the right.

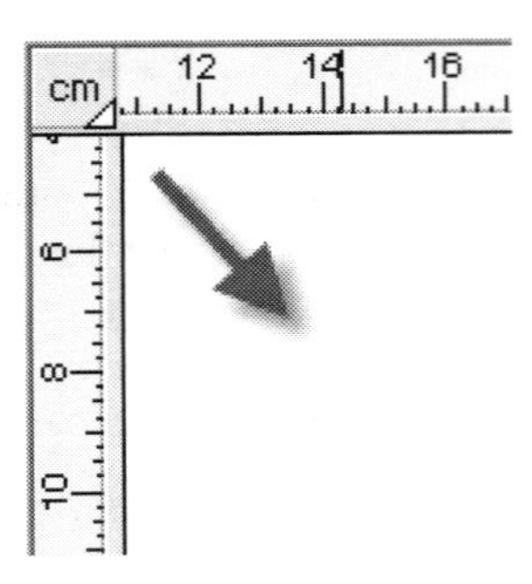

Normally the origin (zero position) of the horizontal or vertical ruler is fixed to the left or top edge of the page, respectively. The small tab ⊿ that is shown on the ruler intersection can be used to set a new ruler origin—simply drag the tab onto the page and release to set the position of your new origin (cross-hair guides and the Hintline toolbar help this positioning). Double click on the ruler intersection to reset the origin back to its default position. All guide positions are recalculated as the origin changes position.

Double-clicking on the ruler intersection at any time automatically makes the rulers jump to any currently selected object. The rulers will always appear above and to the left of the object.

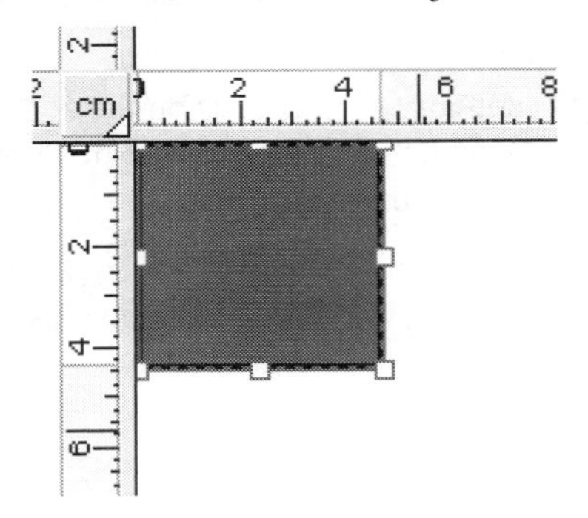

Double-clicking with nothing selected, or double-clicking a second time, resets the rulers so that the origin returns to the top left-hand corner of the page.

Selecting an object or dragging it to a new location will display position information in the HintLine toolbar (relative to the object's top-left corner).

QuickBox: (1.80cm, 1.27cm), 7.67cm x 8.03cm

The figures in brackets give the horizontal and vertical distance moved, the next two figures are the object's width and height.

Guides

Although rulers are useful for gauging the size and position of objects on the page, they do require you to put some work into positioning objects manually. If you want to position objects repeatedly on the same horizontal or vertical boundary then **guides** are much easier.

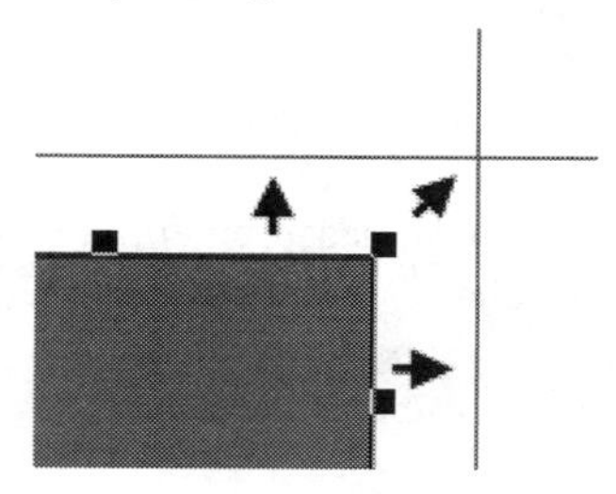

Guides appear as red non-printable vertical or horizontal lines which are "sticky" as long as you have **Snap to Guides** turned on (see below), i.e. a moved object will behave as if it is attracted to a guide as you move it close to the line. Guides also attract the object when you are changing its size.

For snapping, think of objects as being broken into four quadrants. Using the above example, you have to drag from the upper right quadrant of the object towards the guides for effective snapping.

To create a guide:

1. Click on the horizontal or vertical ruler. The horizontal ruler produces a horizontal guide, a vertical ruler a vertical guide.
2. Drag onto the page while fine-tuning the guide into its position. A blue line will appear which turns to red after releasing the mouse button. You can use the rulers and Hintline toolbar to ensure your guide is positioned accurately.

To move, delete and lock guides:

- To move guides, drag the guide wherever you want with the Pointer Tool.
- Dragging and dropping a guide onto its respective ruler will delete it. Guides can also be switched off temporarily or locked from **Tools>Options>Snapping**.

The blue line that you see around the edges of every page is the **margin**. You can set the margin size using the command **File>Page Setup...** or in the context toolbar.

The positioning of new guides, and objects that snap to those guides, is influenced by the snapping grid and its settings.

The snapping grid

The **snapping grid** is another aid to positioning related to the ruler settings. It is a grid of dots, lines or dashes that attract objects in much the same way as guides do.

The spacing of the grid can be set to any number of divisions of the ruler unit using **Tools>Options>Snapping**—enter the number of snap lines per measurement unit you want. Subdivisions can be used to set a snap line to be darker every *n*th line. You can set independent horizontal and vertical divisions. Notice that you cannot change the unit of measurement in this dialog box because this is determined by the rulers.

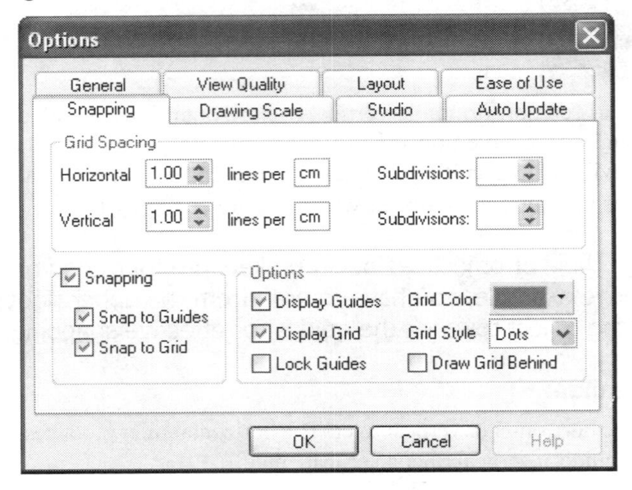

To show the snapping grid, ensure that **Display Grid** is checked (above) or choose **View>Layout Tools** and check the **Snapping Grid** item on the submenu. The grid appears as a matrix of coloured dots, lines or dashes (selected from the **Grid Colour** and **Grid Style** drop-down menus). How many dots you actually see depends on the degree of zoom you have selected but the snapping grid still works at the number of divisions you have selected. For example, if you are working in inches and select 10 lines per inch then the snapping grid will allow you to position an object at $1/10^{th}$ inch increments irrespective of the zoom.

Snapping

When **Snapping** is checked, objects you create, move, or resize will snap to guides, the grid, or both, depending on whether **Snap to Guides** or **Snap to Grid** is checked. For the latter, think of the snapping grid as setting the smallest increment of movement or scaling you can use. With snapping on, you cannot position or size an object between the snapping grid points. For example, if you set the snapping grid to 1 line per centimetre and then move an object you will discover that it appears to jump one whole centimetre at a time.

To turn snapping on and off:

- Check or uncheck the **Snapping** item on the Arrange menu.
  OR
  Choose **Options...** from the Tools menu and select **Snapping**. Check or uncheck the **Snapping** box.

To snap to guides or grid:

- With the Snapping option checked, check the **Snap to Guides** or **Snap to Grid** option in **Tools>Options>Snapping**.

If you find that snapping is a nuisance because it is stopping you from placing objects exactly where you want them, don't just give in and turn snapping off! Snapping is your best aid in getting objects to fit together when you are assembling a drawing. For example, if you align two objects by eye and then zoom in, you will quickly see that they are not accurately aligned at all!

So if you do find snapping bothersome, it may be that you have the grid spacing set too coarsely to allow you the freedom you need in your design. Go to **Tools>Options>Snapping** to set a finer horizontal and/or vertical grid spacing.

Positioning objects by transform

If you want to discover or set the exact position, size and orientation of a selected object click on the **Transform** tab. The tab shows measurements in ruler units.

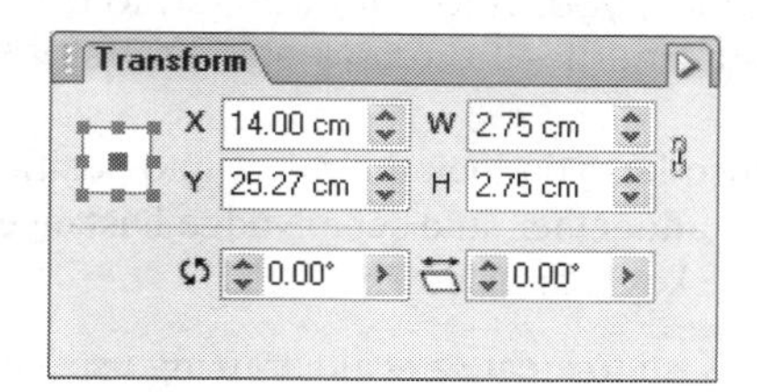

The X and Y **Horizontal** or **Vertical** settings display the current object's position in relation to the ruler's zero point and the currently set anchor point.

To change an object's position:

1. Set the **Anchor point** within the square frame. This sets the point where the object is to be repositioned—from a corner, edge midpoint or centre. For example, to reposition from the object's bottom-left corner, set the Anchor point as:

   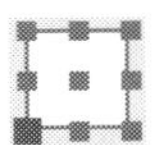

2. Click the small up- or down-arrow "spinwheel" buttons to adjust incrementally.
   OR
   Click in the input box, then press the up or down arrows on the keyboard to change the values shown.
   OR
   Type in an exact value for X and Y and press the Enter key. The higher the respective value, the further the object is moved to the right/bottom of the page.

The object is repositioned according to the currently set Anchor point position.

Measurement Units and Scale

The ruler units used by DrawPlus determine the units displayed on the rulers and the units used when positioning and scaling objects. If you need to change the ruler units, use **Tools>Options...**, click **Layout** and select the desired **Ruler Units** from the list of options.

Right-click your ruler intersection to quickly swap to a different unit of measurement—the rulers and Transform tab are updated instantly.

This also lets you lock the rulers into position or remove them from the display altogether, and set a Nudge Distance for moving or resizing objects with the keyboard arrows.

If you wish to create a scale drawing use **Tools>Options** and click on **Drawing Scale**. Check the **Drawing Scale** option.

The **Scale Drawing** box must be checked in order for the scale drawing options to be available. Adjust the ratio between the Page Distance and Ruler Distance by selecting appropriate values and units for each. Page Distance displays the **page units** that define the document's actual printing dimensions and Ruler Distance shows the onscreen **ruler units** that represent the "real world" objects you're depicting. For new documents, the ratio is always 1:1. When you change the ruler units on the Drawing Scale pane, the unit shown on the Layout pane is simultaneously updated and vice-versa.

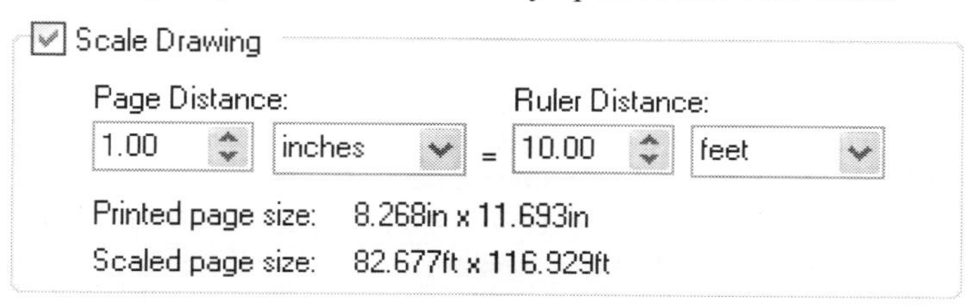

For example, for a house plan you might choose to set a page distance of one inch equivalent to a ruler distance of ten feet. You can adjust either side of the proportion equally. Once you've made the change, ruler markings, dimension lines, and other onscreen units will appear in the selected ruler units and scaled accordingly onto the printed page.

For clarity, the dialog also reports the **printed page size** (in page units) and the **scaled page size** (in "real world" ruler units).

Dimension Lines

DrawPlus lets you add **dimension lines** with text labels showing the distance between two fixed points in a drawing, or the angle formed by three points. For example, you can draw a dimension line along one side of a box, measuring the distance between the two corner points. If you resize the box, the line automatically follows suit, and its label text updates to reflect the new measurement.

The **Dimension Tool** is on the **Line** flyout of the Drawing toolbar. When selected, its Dimensions context toolbar displays tool buttons showing the kind of dimension line each one draws: **Vertical**, **Horizontal**, **Slanted**, or **Angular**. (Slanted lines can be drawn at any angle.)

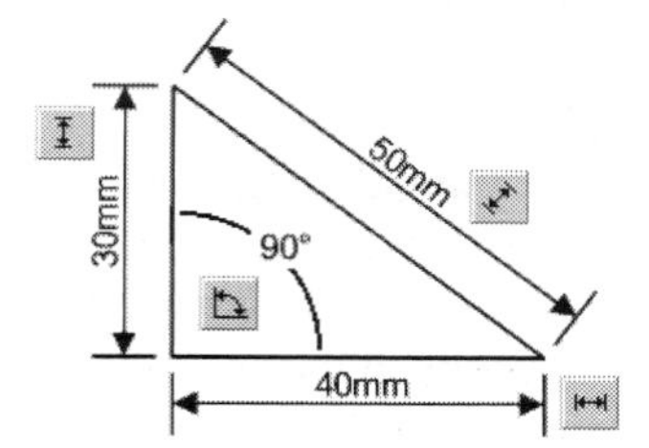

You'll find dimension lines indispensable for creating technical diagrams, floor plans, or any drawing where exact measurements and scale are important. (Look in **start from scratch** on the Startup Wizard for a wide variety of technical templates which you can use to assemble your own diagrams—templates are only available on the DrawPlus 8.0 Resource CD.)

To draw a dimension:

1. Select the **Dimension Tool** from the Drawing toolbar's Line flyout. (The flyout shows the icon of the most recently selected tool.) Choose the appropriate tool option from the Dimension context toolbar.

   Although they can be drawn anywhere on the page, dimension lines are at their most accurate when attached to **connection points** on objects (see p. 105). When you choose the Dimension Tool, connection points (shown as red crosses) become visible when the target object is hovered over. When you move the mouse pointer directly over a connection point, a small box appears around it when a connection can be made.

2. For a **linear dimension** (vertical, horizontal, or slanted), click where you want to start the dimension line (e.g., on a connection point) then drag and release the mouse button where you want to end the line (maybe on another connection point). The illustration below shows the result of dragging between connection points A and B. A pair of parallel **extension lines** appears from the two points. Between the two extension lines, the dimension line and its label "float," awaiting final positioning.

   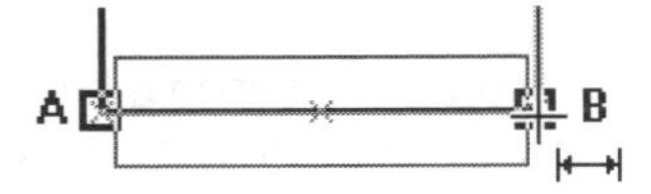

   To complete the dimension line, move the mouse again to position the floating line and its label—note that they respond independently—and click when they are where you want them. (You can always change the positions later.) The dimension line appears.

   OR

   For an **angular dimension**, click a point along one side of the desired angle, then drag and release the mouse button at a point along the other side of the angle (points A and B in the illustration below). Click again at the vertex of the angle (point C below). These three points define the starting and ending sides of the angle. Between the two sides, the angle's arc and its label "float," awaiting final positioning. Click again to position the floating elements.

Angles are measured anticlockwise from the starting to the ending side, so choose your three nodes accordingly.

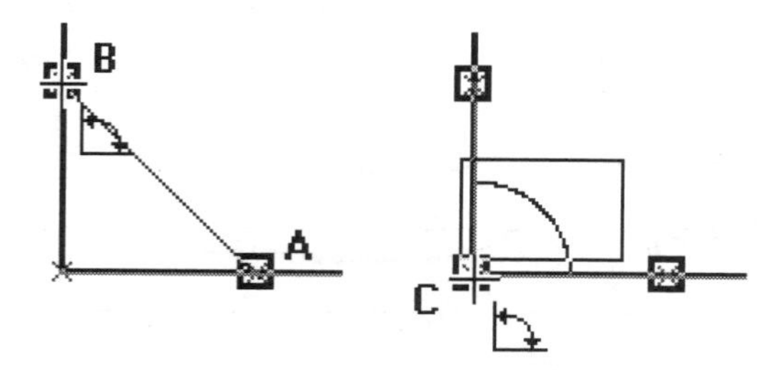

3. To complete the dimension line, move the mouse again to position the floating line or arc and its label—note that they respond independently—and click when they are where you want them. (You can always change the positions later.) The dimension line appears.

Once you've added a dimension line, you can use the **Node Tool** to freely adjust node and label positions if necessary. Use **Format>Character** to change the font, font size, colour and style of the label text. You can also format the line, including line colour, width, style, or adjust the level of precision with the Dimensions context toolbar.

Layers

If you are drawing something simple, you don't really need to make use of layers—you can do all your work on the single layer that every new document has. However, if you're creating something a little more tricky then layers can be a vital aid in separating objects into independent sets. You can think of a layer as a transparent sheet of paper upon which you draw objects. The whole drawing is produced by piling up the layers and viewing all of the objects on all of the layers.

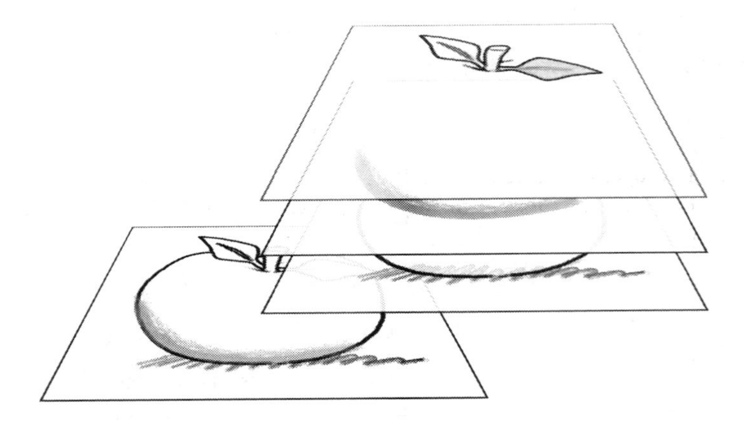

The advantage of using layers is that you can choose which layer you are editing and thus make changes without fear of modifying anything on another layer. By building up your drawing from multiple layers you make it much easier to edit.

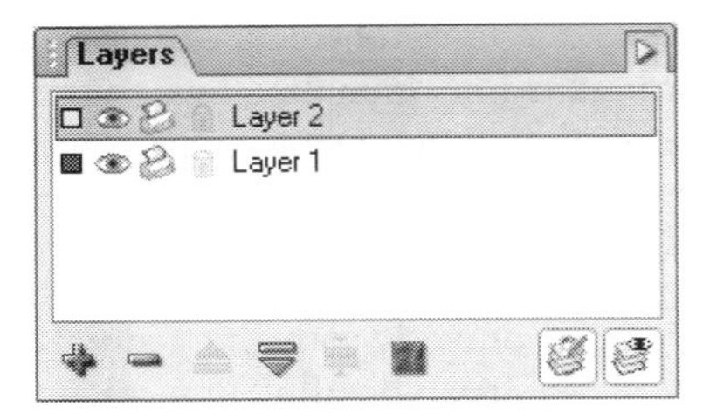

Each layer is situated along with other layers (if present) within a stack on the **Layers** tab—the uppermost layer is applied over any lower layer on the page. The tab allows layers to be created, deleted, reordered and merged.

In order to create a new object on a particular layer, you'll first need to "activate" (switch to) that layer.

To select a particular layer:

- Click a layer name in the **Layers** tab.

Right-clicking a layer name displays a menu of layer-related actions, and can access layer properties for that particular layer.

To display the Layers tab:

- Go to **View>Studio Tabs** and select the **Layers** tab, if the tab is not visible.

Adding, removing and rearranging layers

To add a new layer to the drawing:

1. In the Layers tab, click the **Add Layer** button.
2. A new layer is created above the topmost layer in the stack. You can name the layer something meaningful, or you just accept the default names Layer 2, Layer 3, and so on—use right-click and select **Layer Properties...** to rename.
3. Use the Layer Properties dialog to make the layer hidden, non-printable or locked if needed.
4. Click **OK**.

To delete a layer:

- In the Layers tab, select the layer's name and click the **Delete Layer** button.

You can move layers up or down in the stacking order to place their objects in front or behind those on other layers, move objects to specific layers, and even merge layers.

To move a layer in the stacking order:

- In the Layers tab, select the layer's entry, then click the **Move Forward** or **Move Back** button to move the layer up or down in the list, respectively.

OR

- Drag the selected layer to a new position in the frame stack.

Remember that objects on layers are drawn in the order in which the layers were initially added to the Layers tab. Put another way: the bottom layer in the Layers tab stack is drawn first then the second bottom, third bottom etc. A background layer should be the bottom layer in the Layers tab stack.

To merge a layer:

1. Activate the layer you want to merge **to** by clicking its entry. The layer is highlighted in blue. (Note that the active layer becomes uppermost in the workspace.)
2. With the **Ctrl** key pressed, select a single or multiple layers that you want to merge (the layers are framed with a blue border).
3. Click the **Merge** button. The contents of the merged layer(s) appear on the active layer.

Managing objects on layers

To add objects to a particular layer:

- When drawn, objects are added to the selected layer automatically. This is why it is a good idea to check which layer you are currently working on!

To select objects on a particular layer:

- In the Layers tab, click the chosen layer and click the object. Selection handles will appear on the object.

Initially, objects which are on layers that are not selected are also visible, but you may find that you can't select an object as it is on a different layer. This can be slightly confusing at first as you frantically click on an object to no effect! But of course, you can change this state of affairs.

To select any object on any layer:

1. Select a layer entry in the Layers tab.
2. Click the **Edit All Layers** button. You can then select and edit any object irrespective of the layer selected.

To view objects on only one layer at a time, uncheck **View All Layers** in the Layers tab.

To move an object to another layer:

- Select the object, right-click and choose **Move Object to Layer**. From the dialog, select the specific destination layer.
  OR
- Select the object, right-click and choose **Move Object to Active Layer**. The object moves to whichever layer was previously active.
  OR

- Select the object, and choose **Move To Layer>Move Forward One Layer** and **Move Back One Layer**, in the **Arrange>Layers** menu. This moves the object to the layer above or below its current layer.

Layer properties

Layer properties allow you to rename an existing layer, and make layers invisible, non-printable and/or locked. An object's selection handle colour can also be defined based on its current layer.

If you delete a layer, all of the objects on it are lost! So if you want to keep any of them, move them to another layer first.

To set layer properties:

1. Display the Layers tab.
2. Select desired settings for each selected layer.

- Click/unclick the **Visible** icon to show/hide the layer and any objects on it.
- Click/unclick the **Printable** column to include/exclude the layer in printouts. Non-printing layers are handy "for information only."
- Click/unclick the **Locked** column to allow/prevent objects on the layer from being selected and edited.
- To set the **Selection handle colour**, click the **Colour selection** button and choose a colour from the palette (click **More Colours...** for a wider choice). Assigning different handle colours to layers means that you can quickly verify that a pasted object has gone to the correct layer, i.e. the selection handles of an object on a layer always adopts the Selection handle colour assigned to the layer.

Tutorial Resources

For more experience with the tools and techniques covered in this chapter, we recommend these PDF-based tutorials (go to **Help>Tutorials** in DrawPlus):

Try this tutorial...	For practice with these tools and techniques...
Explore the DrawPlus Gallery	Scaling Drawings
Work With Line Tools	Using Guides
Create a Wine Glass	Page Manager, Working with Multiple Pages
Making a Clock Face	Creating and Managing Layers

Jump between your PDF tutorials and DrawPlus with **Alt-Tab**.

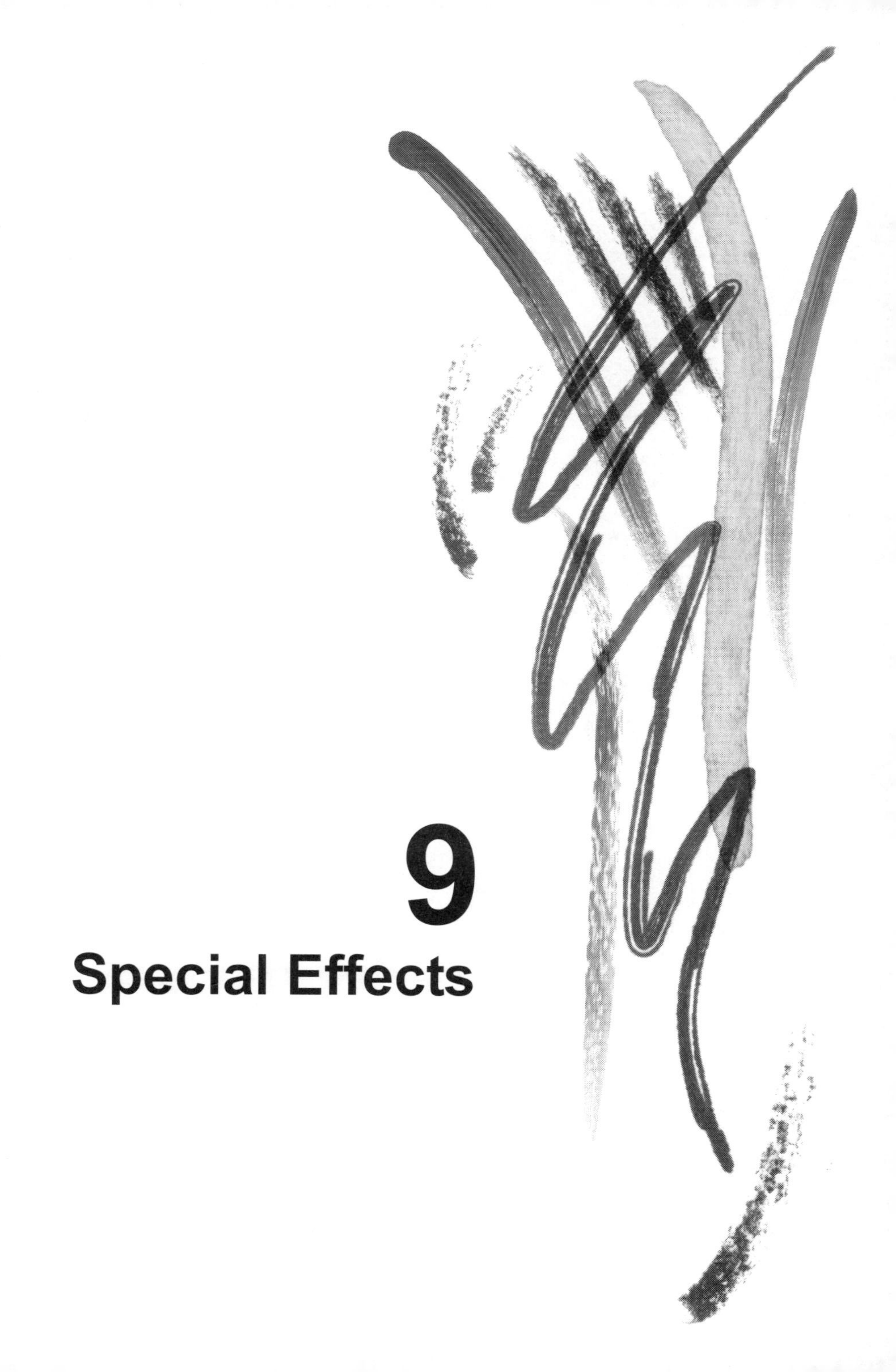

9
Special Effects

Introduction

DrawPlus Design templates and samples offer some starting points and incentives to create original designs of your own, but, for the most part, you will have to use your own level of creativity to maximum effect. It's therefore very important that you know as much as you can about all the tools at your disposal. Seeing how the tools work, and then trying them yourself, will literally open your eyes to new possibilities—and spur your own creativity.

In this chapter we'll spend some time looking at tools we may just have mentioned in passing, explore some new ones, and offer some examples of how to "put it all together" for effects you might not have thought possible.

Text Effects

Although you might think of text as just being the mundane, informative part of your design, it often has a key role to play in setting the visual tone. The basic appearance of the letters is controlled by the typeface that you select. A typeface is a family of fonts in different sizes and typestyles—bold, italic, etc. It's important to understand font choices as a starting point, but with DrawPlus, you can achieve typographic results that go far beyond the limits of particular fonts.

Font choices

serif The "traditional" serif fonts have short lines at the end of each longer line that makes up the letter, e.g.

Times New Roman a serif font

sans-serif look modern, mechanical, and clean, e.g.

Arial a sans-serif font

decorative typefaces designed for maximum visual impact, e.g.

Sprint SF a decorative font

With DrawPlus, selecting a font is easy and you can preview the large number of fonts directly from the Text context toolbar.

However, try to remember the following rules:

- Don't use too many fonts. It makes a design look messy and difficult to understand.
- Make sure that important text is readable. Never sacrifice legibility for design.
- Choose fonts that work together. Look at your entire design and see if any font looks as if it belongs to another drawing.

Free text vs. shape text

As detailed in Chapter 6, free text and shape text share many of the same properties—you can even detach shape text from its container as a free text object! In most instances, you can just choose whichever format is most convenient for you. But keep in mind that each type of text has some unique advantages.

- In general, **free text** is better suited to decorative or fancy typographic design. For example, free text characters possess line properties, whereas shape text characters can only accept a fill. And because free text objects are independent, rather than "belonging" to a shape, they can be manipulated with the Curve Text Wizard (see below) and take other special effects.
- On the other hand, it's precisely because **shape text** belongs to its container that it lends itself so well to blocks of body text where shape and flow contribute to the overall layout. You'd have a hard time squeezing several paragraphs of free text into some shapes—and an even harder time trying to alter the design later on.

Arranging letters

Whether you're creating free text or shape text, once you have selected a font you have additional choices as to how to arrange individual letters or groups of letters.

Most of the time you can let DrawPlus set the distances between letters and words, but sometimes it is worth moving a pair of letters closer or further apart to improve their appearance. This is called **kerning**. The **Kern Text** option is normally switched on in the Character dialog.

For free text, you can also tweak letter positions by hand.

1. Select free text with the **Node Tool**.
2. Drag the character's square handle to where you want it; rotate it using the blue rotation arm that appears. The letters "a" and "s" have been raised in the example below— "a" has also been rotated. This is great for creating special effect and logos and the text can still be edited!

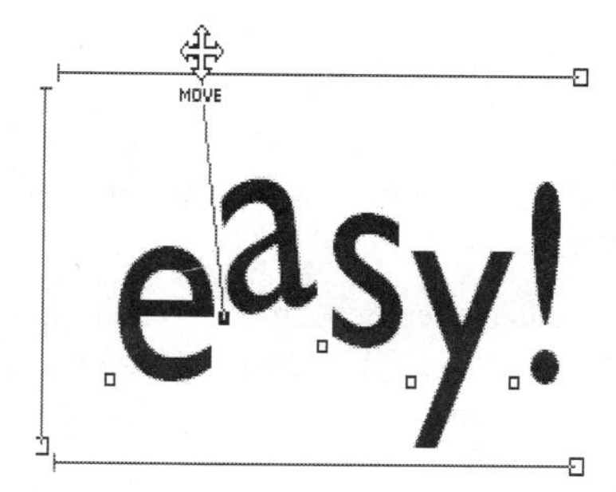

To make the job easier, hold down the **Shift** key after selecting a letter to move. This constrains it to move only horizontally or vertically. If you want to move a group of letters, select them one at a time with the **Shift** key held down.

Another very simple and often overlooked technique is to vary the point size within a line of text. You can do this onscreen or via the Edit Text window by selecting just the characters you want to change... in this example, just the exclamation point:

Text on a curve

Being able to move each character to any location is a powerful way of arranging text. However, for some special effects you will want the text to follow a regular path such as a circle, spiral, arc, or on a drawn curve.

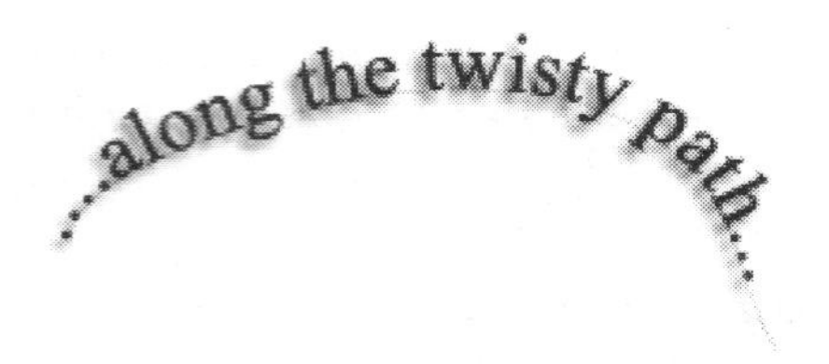

You can fit free text to a wide range of regular paths using the **Curve Text Wizard**. You can either add existing text to a series of preset paths or add new text (via the wizard) to a previously selected object.

To create text on a curve:

1. If you want to use an existing text or shape object, select the object first. Otherwise, you can enter text or pick a shape in the wizard.
2. Go to **Tools>Curve Text Wizard**.
3. After the first screen, enter text to be placed on the curve. This is not shown when text has already selected on the page.
4. In the second screen, if an object or outline has already been selected the **Use Current Selection** option will be checked. Uncheck if you want your text to flow along one of the available preset curves then pick a curve on which the text will be placed.

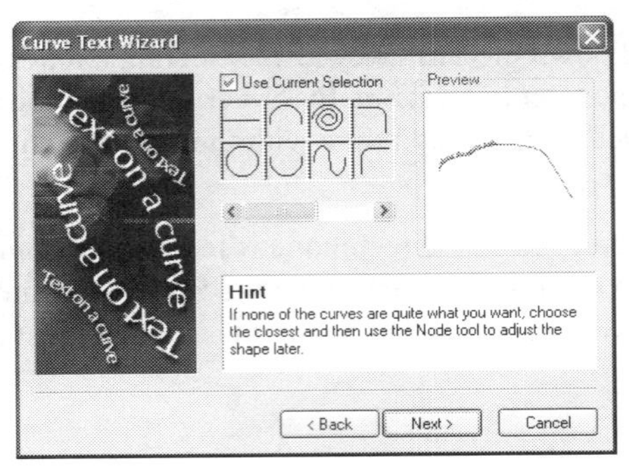

5. Close the wizard. This will display your text arranged on the curve, line or shape.

2D Filter Effects

DrawPlus provides a variety of **filter effects** that you can use to transform any object. The standard or 2D filter effects are especially well adapted to text, as shown here:

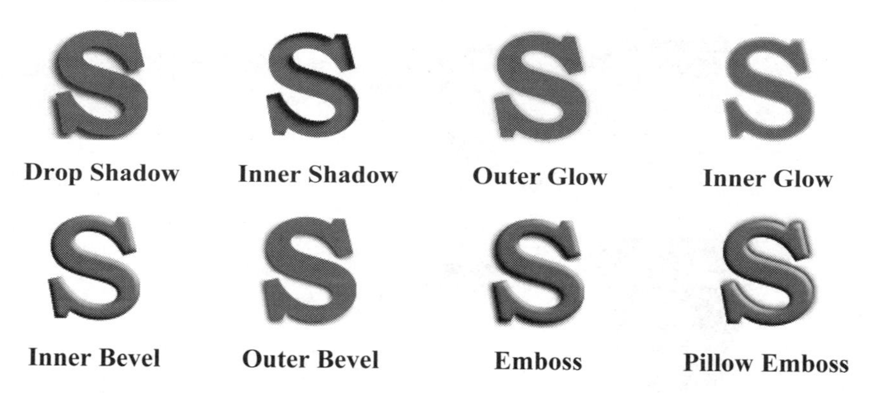

An object's 2D filter effect can be applied or edited singularly via a **Filter Effects** dialog, equipped with a branching checklist of available effects. Multiple effects can also be applied cumulatively. See DrawPlus help for full details on each effect.

To apply a shadow, glow, bevel, or emboss filter effect:

1. Select an object and choose **Filter Effects...** from the Format menu. The Filter Effects dialog appears.

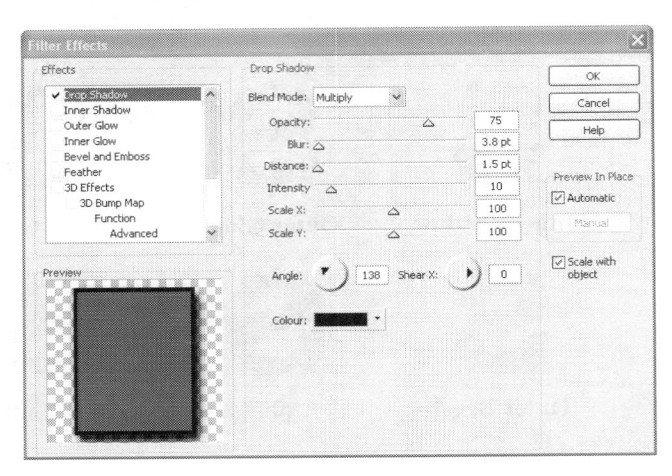

2. To apply one or more effects, check appropriate boxes in the list at left. Select an effect name to display the dialog specific to that effect.

3. For Shadow and Glow effects, choose a blend mode from the list. Click the **Colour** swatch to change the shadow colour or base highlight from its default (either white or black)
   OR
   For Bevel and Emboss effects, choose a Highlight blend mode from the list and set the Opacity slider. Click the **Colour** swatch and change the highlight colour from its default (white). Then choose a Shadow blend mode, opacity, and colour (default black).

4. To adjust the properties of a specific effect, select its name and vary the dialog controls. Adjust the sliders or enter specific values to vary the combined effect. (You can also select a slider and use the keyboard arrows.) Options differ from one effect to another.

5. Check the **Scale with object** box if you want the effect to adjust in proportion to any change in the object's size. With the box unchecked, the effect's extent remains fixed if you resize the object.

6. Click **OK** to apply the effect to the selected object, or **Cancel** to abandon changes.

Feathering

Feathering is a filter effect that adds a soft or blurry edge to any object. It's great for blending single objects into a composition, vignetted borders on photos, and much more. You can apply feathering in conjunction with other filter effects.

The Shadow Tool

Another way to apply a drop shadow is to choose the **Shadow Tool** on the Drawing toolbar, then drag from the object.

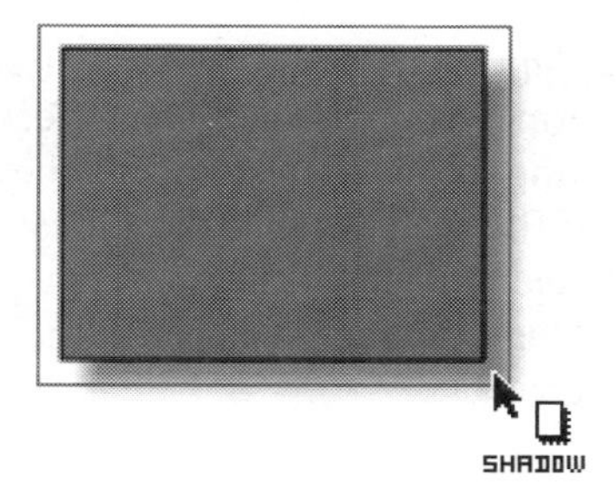

You can continue to click and drag the shadow to adjust its position. To toggle between a simple and a slanted shadow, press **Ctrl** and begin dragging. To change a shadow's colour, choose the Shadow Tool and click a thumbnail on the Studio's Colour tab. As long as the Shadow Tool is selected, colours are applied to the shadow, not to the object.

Notice the context toolbar appear when you selected the Shadow Tool? This allows the shadow properties to be altered, including the blend mode, opacity, blurring and X/Y shearing.

Shadows applied using the Shadow Tool can be removed at any time with a simple double-click while the Shadow Tool is selected!

3D Filter Effects

3D filter effects create the impression of a textured surface, and are a bit more complex than their 2D cousins (see the previous section). Actually, there's an easy way to get started with them: simply display the **Effects tab** and preview its gallery thumbnails.

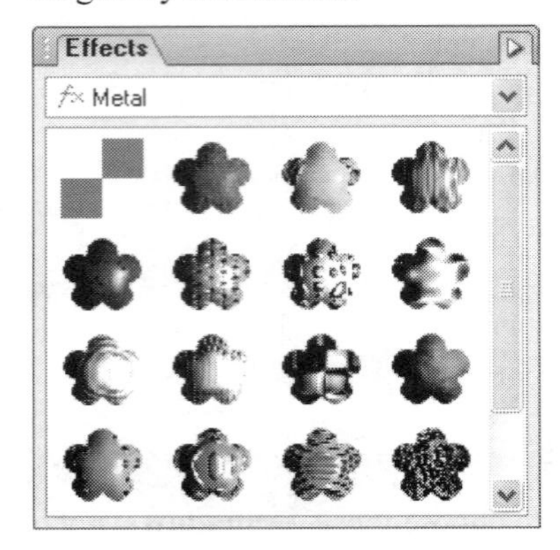

There you'll see a variety of remarkable 3D surface and texture presets in various categories (glass, metal, wood, etc.). Click any thumbnail to apply it to the selected object. Assuming the object has some colour on it to start with, you'll see an instant result! Note that none of these effects will work on objects using the "Instant 3D" effect as described in the next section. Nor will they "do" anything to an unfilled object—you'll need to have a fill there to see the difference they make!

Alternatively, to create your own or to customize one of the 3D filter effects above, choose **Filter Effects...** from the Format menu. In the Filter Effects dialog, check the **3D Effects** and **3D Lighting** boxes (if customizing they will already be checked). The master settings of Blur and Depth make a great difference; you can click the "+" button to unlink them for independent adjustment. As for 3D Lighting, without a "light source" switched on, the depth information in the effect wouldn't be visible.

You might be wondering why all the 3D effects seem to have "map" in their name. So what is a map, anyway? Actually, it's the key to understanding how these effects work. Let's call it a channel of information overlaid on the image, storing values for each underlying image pixel. It's as if the object were printed on a flexible sheet, which is flat to start with. Each 3D effect employs a map that interacts with the underlying layer's image to create the impression of a textured surface.

Bump Maps superimpose depth information for a bumpy, peak-and-valley effect. Using the flexible sheet metaphor, the bump map adds up-and-down contours and the image "flexes" along with these bumps, like shrink-wrap, while a light from off to one side accentuates the contours.

Pattern Maps contribute colour variations using a choice of blend modes and transparency, for realistic (or otherworldly!) depictions of wood grain, marbling, and blotches or striations of all kinds.

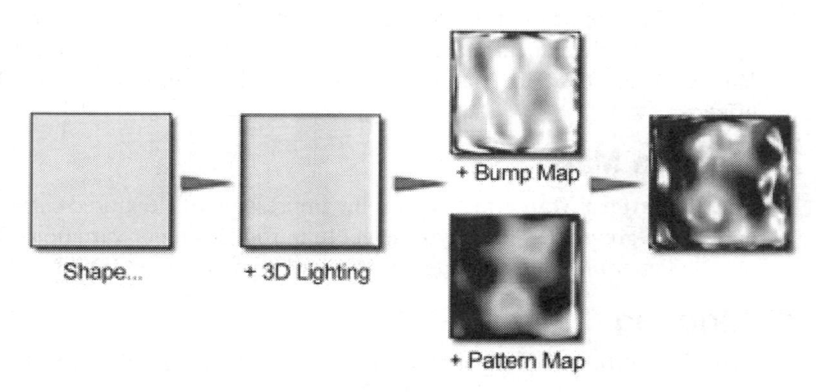

You'll notice that Bump Maps and Pattern Maps come in two varieties: "2D" and "3D." Don't be misled! These are all three-dimensional effects; the distinction has to do with how each one achieves its result. With the "3D" Bump Maps and Pattern Maps, you first pick a mathematical function. With the "2D" variants, you begin by selecting a bitmap from a gallery. The function-based maps include data about the interior of the "space," while the bitmap-based maps describe only surface characteristics.

It is possible to combine multiple 3D filter effects, as in the illustration above. The effects are applied cumulatively, in a standard "pipeline" sequence: 3D Bump > 2D Bump > 3D Pattern > 2D Pattern > 3D Lighting.

The procedures for applying 3D Filter Effects are covered in the DrawPlus Help but here's a quick review of each effect type.

3D Bump Map

The **3D Bump Map** effect creates the impression of a textured surface by applying a mathematical function you select to add depth information, for a peak-and-valley effect. You can use 3D Bump Map in conjunction with one or more additional 3D filter effects—but not with a 2D Bump Map.

2D Bump Map

The **2D Bump Map** effect creates the impression of a textured surface by applying a greyscale bitmap you select to add depth information, for a peak-and-valley effect. You can use 2D Bump Map in conjunction with one or more additional 3D filter effects—but not with a 3D Bump Map.

3D Pattern Map

The **3D Pattern Map** effect creates the impression of a textured surface by applying a mathematical function you select to introduce colour variations. You can use 3D Pattern Map in conjunction with one or more other 3D filter effects.

2D Pattern Map

The **2D Pattern Map** effect creates the impression of a textured surface by applying a greyscale bitmap you select to introduce colour variations. You can use 2D Pattern Map in conjunction with one or more other 3D filter effects.

3D Lighting

The **3D Lighting** effect works in conjunction with other 3D effects to let you vary the surface illumination and reflective properties.

Dimensionality (Instant 3D)

Using the **Instant 3D** feature, you can easily transform flat shapes and text into three-dimensional objects with precise control over settings like extrusion, rotation, lighting, and texture. (Note that Instant 3D doesn't work on objects already using one or more of the filter effects described above.)

To add dimensionality:

1. Select an object and choose **Instant 3D** from the Drawing toolbar. The Instant 3D dialog appears, with the **3D Effects** entry selected at the left.

2. Change your 3D effect options for Extrusion, Lens, X Rotation, Y Rotation, and Z Rotation. **Extrusion** is an especially important setting—it determines the extra thickness or Z-axis dimensionality added to the object. **Lens** widens or narrows the field of view, while the various rotation controls let you swivel the object in all three dimensions.

3. If required, apply other settings—all contributing to the 3D effect applied to the selected object, i.e.
   - **Bevel** - lets you carve or sculpt the edges of the added (extruded) region, for a convex, concave, or slanted appearance.
   - **Light** - determine the direction and quality of an imaginary light source, which varies the shading that produces a convincing depth effect.
   - **Render** - experiment with different settings for the best performance on your particular machine.
   - **Texture** - vary settings to determine how a radial or Bitmap fill pattern is projected onto the object.

4. Click **OK** when you've made your choices.

See the DrawPlus Help for more details.

You can also drag or **Shift-**drag on the object in the preview window to rotate or extrude it, respectively.

Envelopes

An **envelope** distortion is one that you can apply to any object to change its shape without having to edit its nodes. To understand how an envelope affects the shape of an object, imagine it drawn on a rectangular rubber sheet which is stretched to the outline of the selected envelope. As you might expect, this is a very powerful feature for special effects—and not only for text.

To apply an envelope:

1. Select the object or group of objects you want to distort.

2. Choose **Tools>Envelope Wizard**. As the first step, the Wizard gives you the choice of applying the distortion either to the currently selected object or to some new text. The next step lets you browse through the possible envelope shapes and preview their effect.

Envelope Wizard

Choose an envelope:

Preview

Envelope

Hint

If none of the envelope shapes are what you want, choose the closest and then use the Node tool to adjust the shape later.

< Back | Next > | Cancel

3. Select the envelope you want to use.
4. Clicked **Finish** in the final step, you will see your object distort to match the preview.

You can select the Node Tool to allow you to edit the selected object's outline (see Editing Curves on p. 73).

An alternative to using the Envelope Wizard is to use the **Envelope Tool** on the Drawing toolbar. This tool permits an object's nodes to be moved in order to create custom envelopes or to allow preset envelopes to be applied to the selected object. The displayed context toolbar, shown while the tool is active, offers various options to customize the envelope—envelope shape, line colour, weight, and style can all be altered.

The **User Defined** envelope in the context bar's **Preset Envelopes** retrieves the last drawn custom envelope shape used in your current DrawPlus session.

3D Perspective

The **Perspective Tool**, like the Envelope Tool, produces an overall shape distortion. But while the Envelope effect stretches the object as if it were printed on a rubber sheet, Perspective gives you the visual impression of a flat surface being tilted in space, with an exaggerated front/back size differential. Using the Node Tool, you can achieve just about any freeform viewpoint, making this a versatile effect for both text and shapes. You can achieve a similar result using Shear and other tools—but only with considerably more effort!

To apply perspective:

1. Select an object and click the **Perspective Tool** on the Drawing toolbar. Effects are applied immediately and the Node Tool is activated.
2. Either:

- Drag the "3D" cursor over the selected object or drag the special adjustment slider handle left or right to see it respond by tilting in all sorts of orientations. Use Undo if you're not happy with a particular adjustment.

OR

- From the context toolbar, select an item from **Perspective Presets** flyout closest to the effect you're after. The first item, Pre Defined perspective, retrieves the last drawn custom perspective shape used in your current DrawPlus session. You can still use the 3D cursor and handles for adjusting perspective.

Roughening

The Roughen Tool lets you selectively distort an object's outline, for a jagged appearance. The effect can lend cartoon-like flair to ordinary text or give QuickShapes an irregular appearance ...in fact apply it whenever it seems to suit the mood of the design.

To apply Roughening:

1. Select the **Roughen Tool** from the Drawing toolbar.
2. Drag the cursor up or down on a selected object. The more you drag, the rougher the object's outline becomes.

Note that *only* the outline is affected and there's no internal distortion—so if the object is using a bitmap fill, for example, the fill remains intact.

Blends

Blends enable you to "morph" any shape into any other shape in a specified number of steps. If the two shapes are separated in space, each step creates an intermediate shape, a kind of morphing effect. The result is a group object (lower image).

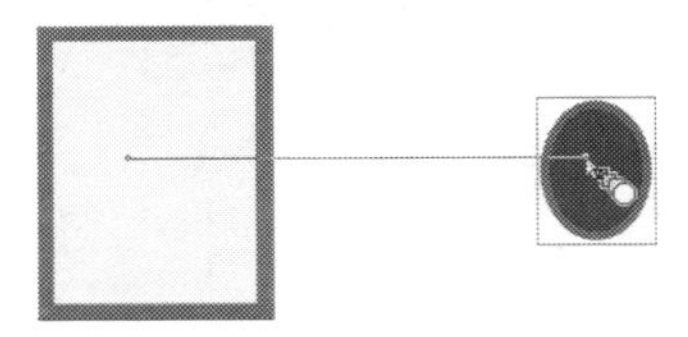

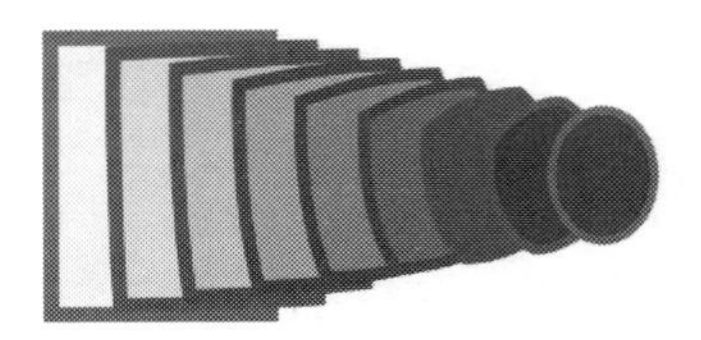

To apply a blend:

1. Select the Blend Tool on the Drawing toolbar.
2. Hover over the object to display a blue bounding box and Blend cursor.
3. Click and drag the cursor, drawing a line as you go, to your destination point (this must be on an object) and release.
4. In the dialog, enter the number of "morph" steps to be taken between both points and click **OK**.

Note that the colour, line properties and transparency all change along with the object shape during the blend process.

If the starting objects are in the same place, the results can be especially interesting. For example, two Quick Stars of differing size and colour can be overlaid so that the smaller star sits inside the large star (you may want to align their centres). Blending such objects creates impressive results.

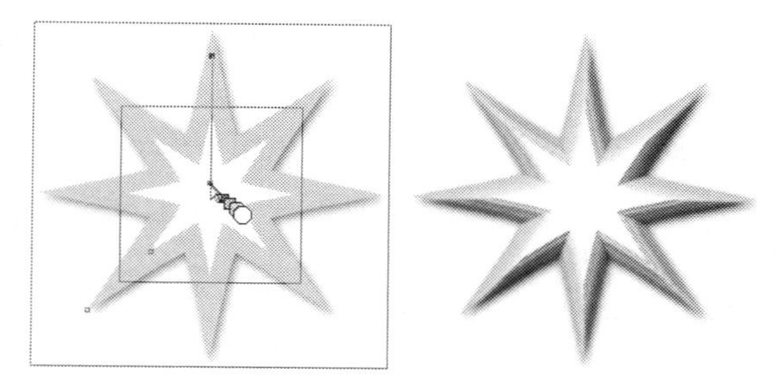

If the two objects you want to blend are quite close together, making selection with the Blend Tool difficult, you can begin by selecting them both with the Pointer Tool, then using **Tools>Blend** to apply the effect.

Try the same effect with text for exciting results!

Chain Lines

A **chain** (or **chain line**) is a decorative line incorporating one or more individual DrawPlus objects arrayed along its length—rather like a border motif, but with all the freeform adaptability of a plain line. You can choose from the wide assortment of chain lines, edit their properties to suit your needs, or create your own chains from scratch. Apply chains to lines, curves, QuickShapes, filled shapes, even text... anywhere you want to instantly introduce repeating elements.

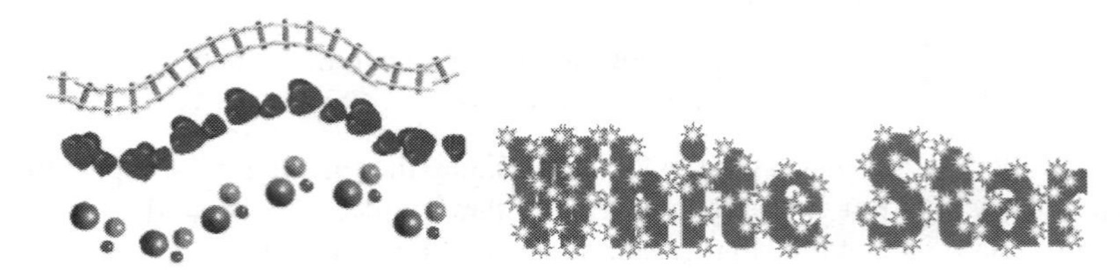

To apply a chain line:

1. Switch on the Studio's **Line Styles** tab from the **Studio Tabs** option on the View menu. The tab is switched off by default.
2. Select a chain line category (all except "Plain") from the drop-down menu.
3. Choose and drag your chain line thumbnail onto an object (or select the object first, then click the thumbnail).

While the pre-supplied chains in the gallery offer plenty of possibilities, it's quite easy to create your own by "stringing together" one or more DrawPlus objects, adding one selection at a time to the chain.

To create your own chain line:

1. Draw an assembly of objects (chain elements) that will make up your chain line. It's best to get all necessary sizing, fill and line properties correct before adding to your chain line.
2. Select all elements that will make up the chain.
3. Pick a suitable chain line category, or create your own by right-clicking on any existing chain line and choosing **Add Category**.
4. At the top of the tab, click the **Create chain** button. The chain will be created as the last entry in the category, with all elements present in the chain.

Plain line properties like thickness, line style, and line end do not apply to chain lines.

To edit a chain line:

- If you want to add an additional element, then select the element on the page, right-click the gallery thumbnail and choose **Add Element**.
- To edit a chain line's properties, right-click either an existing chain line on your page or the gallery thumbnail and choose **Format>Chain Line** or **Edit Chain...**, respectively.
  - On the dialog's **Options** tab, change the **Scale** amount to adjust the overall proportions of the chain's elements with respect to the line or shape. You can fine-tune such properties as **Rotation**, **Spacing**, **Offset**, and **Order**.
  - The dialog's **Elements** tab lets you rearrange the sequence of elements in a chain. To shift an element, click to select it, then click the **Shift Left** or **Shift Right** button. To delete a selected element, click the **Delete** button.

Transforms

The **Transform** feature lets you make multiple copies of one or more selected objects, with a transformation applied to each successive copy in the series. Transforms are a great way to generate elements for an Animation sequence involving rotation or directional changes (see p. 199).

To create a transform:

1. Select an object then choose **Transform...** from the Tools menu.
2. From the dialog, specify the type of transformation (rotation and/or scaling), the number of copies, and a positional offset between copies. For example, to create a shell shape from a simple circle, you can choosing 2° rotation, 93% scaling, 50 copies, and an X offset of 0.5cm.

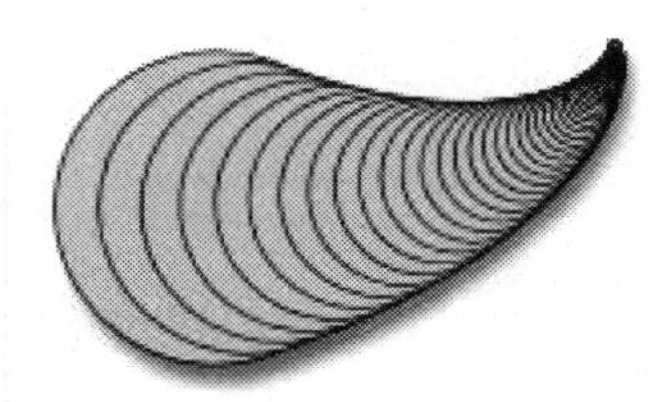

You can reposition one or more selected objects by using the Transform tab (see p. 167).

Contouring

The **Create Contour** function lets you reproduce a single object slightly larger or smaller than the original, for perspective or shape effects. For example, you can quickly create outlines around text.

To apply contours:

1. Select the object you want to reproduce, then choose **Create Contour...** from the Tools menu.
2. Use the dialog to specify the degree of difference (Small, Medium, Large or Custom) and position of the new object with respect to the original (i.e., Outside or Inside).
3. Click **OK**. A reduced copy appears in front of the original object; an enlarged copy appears behind it.

The new object always has a black line and white fill for visibility, but it's selected so you can apply a custom line and fill right away.

Tutorial Resources

For more experience with the tools and techniques covered in this chapter, we recommend these PDF-based tutorials (go to **Help>Tutorials** in DrawPlus):

Try this tutorial...	For practice with these tools and techniques...
Create Filter Effects/Create a Glass Effect/ Create Raised and Sunken Buttons	Bevel and Emboss Filter Effects
Create 3D Effects	Instant 3D Effect
Create a Chain Line	Chain Lines
Create an 8-Ball	Cropping
Create Shadows and Clouds/ Create Raised and Sunken Buttons	Shadow Filter Effects, Feathering
Create a Warped Film Strip	Envelope Wizard
Create Text on a Curve	Text on a Curve
Add Perspective to a Web button	Applying Perspective
Blend and Animate Objects	Blend Tool
Create a Wine Glass	Lighting effects with Transparency

Jump between your PDF tutorials and DrawPlus with **Alt-Tab**.

10
Animation and Web Graphics

Introduction

DrawPlus has a lot to offer if you're producing either static or animated graphics for Web pages. It's hard to overstate the advantages of scalable vector graphics, which let you work at any level of detail and revise any portion of the image. On top of that, DrawPlus adds export optimization and browser preview capabilities, so you're assured of getting the results you want while minimizing file sizes. This chapter explains how to create animations and how to add hyperlinking and onscreen interactivity to things like Web buttons and menus.

Animation Basics

The term "animation" can cover everything from flip-books to Disney movies. We'll focus on what DrawPlus does best: create animated GIFs or AVIs for Web pages.

Bear in mind that DrawPlus isn't an animation *editor* as such. You can preview your work and export it to an animation file format but you can't actually import or play back content in that format. DrawPlus is a powerful vector graphics program, and the control that gives you over objects and special effects makes it ideal for generating animations. The animations will play back on almost any Windows system without extra software. However, if you plan to incorporate the animations in a Web page or video, you'll need a separate program to handle those productions—consider Serif's MoviePlus!

What is animation? Like movies and TV, it's a way of creating the illusion of motion by displaying a series of still pictures, rapidly enough to fool the eye—or more accurately, the brain. Professional animators have developed a whole arsenal of techniques for character animation—rendering human (and animal) movement in a convincing way. We can leave most of this to the experts. Web graphics, as a rule, are relatively small (mainly to keep file size to a minimum) and most often involve shape and colour transformations rather than realistic portrayals.

Creating an animation

With DrawPlus, it's easy to create animated GIFs and AVI movies with multiple images, stored as frames that a Web browser can play back in series. DrawPlus's Animation Mode provides an Animation toolbar and a Frames tab so you can create individual frames, preview animations, and export as a standalone GIF or AVI file.

To begin a new animation from scratch:

- Choose **New>New Animation** from the File menu. A new document window opens in Animation mode.

To convert an existing drawing to animation:

1. Choose **Convert to Animation** from the File menu. You'll be prompted to save changes (if any) to your existing drawing.
2. Select **Yes** to save your work, **No** to convert to an animation or **Cancel** to continue working on your current drawing.

Once your work has been converted to animation, it cannot be converted back to a drawing—so be sure to save the drawing if you'll need to use it again.

With the exception of drawings with a border (drawn with the Border Wizard), all layers in your drawing will be combined into a single frame. The border will be placed in its own automatically created background frame named "Paper".

Working with animation frames

In most cases, your new animation will have a single frame which is displayed in the Frames tab. This tab bears an uncanny resemblance to the Layers tab. In fact while in Animation mode, the Frames tab replaces the Layers tab so that you can manage your animation frames from within the tab as you would for layers. For easier accessibility, you can also manage frames in your Frames tab by using the Animation toolbar. This is positioned in the lower left of your workspace (Animation mode only). The toolbar mirrors the functions available in the Frames tab.

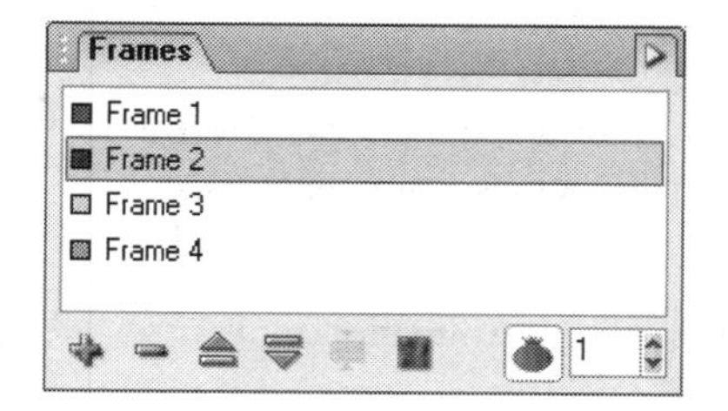

Use the Frames tab (top) or Animation toolbar (bottom) if you want to add, delete or reorder frames, and access individual frame properties. The Animation toolbar lets you quickly jump to the next and previous frame.

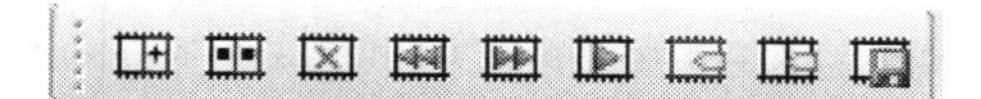

To create new frames, you can either clone the current frame or generate a blank frame. Choose to clone if you will be reusing the current frame's contents with a transformation of some kind (the most common way of simulating change or movement). Either way, the new frame now becomes the current frame.

To clone the current frame as a new frame:

- Display the Frames tab, right-click your chosen frame to be cloned and select **Clone Frame**.
  OR

  Select a frame in the Frames tab, and choose **Clone Frame** from the Animation toolbar.

The cloned frame appears in the Frames tab below existing frames.

To generate a new blank frame:

- Display the Frames tab and click the **New Frame** button.
  OR

  Choose **New Frame** from the Animation toolbar.

The new frame appears in the Frames tab below existing frames.

To view or edit a particular frame:

- Select a frame in the Frames tab. Objects on that frame can then be edited.
  OR

  Use the **Next Frame** or **Previous Frame** button on the Animation toolbar.

To rename a frame:

- Select the frame in the Frames tab, right-click and choose **Frame Properties....** In the **Name:** field, type in a new frame name.
  OR
  Select **Frame Properties** button on the Animation toolbar.

To change frame sequence:

- In the Frames tab, click **Move Back** or **Move Forward** button to move the selected frame backwards or forwards in the frame sequence, respectively.

OR

- Drag the selected frame to a new position in the frame stack.

Remember that the top frame in the Frames tab is displayed first in the sequence then the second top, third top, etc.

To delete a frame:

- Select the frame in the Frames tab and choose the **Delete Frame** button on the Frames tab or Animation toolbar.

Background frames

The Frame Properties dialog, accessible from the Frames tab or Animation toolbar, lets you designate any frame as a **background frame**, which will remain visible while other frames animate "over" it.

Typically, this would be the first frame in your sequence—for example, a background object (sun, tree, mountains or other landscape features) that remains static while an object (a stick man) is animated in the foreground.

You can apply a background frame as a positioning aid while you're creating an animation and then delete it before exporting—arcs, paths, or shapes could all be drawn as aids.

Borders

As well as creating background frames from scratch, DrawPlus lets you use borders to enhance your animations as well. The object is placed on a special bottom frame called the **Paper** frame. This will automatically be designated as a Background frame, on the assumption you'll want it visible behind the other frames.

Overlay frames

The Frame Properties dialog also lets you designate a frame as an **overlay frame** whose non-drawn or blank portions become "transparent," so the contents of the preceding frame show through. The effect is rather like having onion skinning turned on, except that the overlay property carries over to the final animation. The main advantage is saving you the time of having to copy or redraw objects in a series where each frame builds cumulatively on previous frames.

Onion skinning

Onion skinning is a standard animation technique derived from cel animation, where transparent sheets enable the artist to see through to preceding frame(s). It's useful for enabling precise registration and controlling object movement from frame to frame.

You can turn the feature on or off (the default is off) as needed, and set the number of previous frames that will be visible (normally one).

To turn onion skinning on or off:

1. Display the Frames tab.
2. Click the **Onion Skinning** button to turn onion skinning on.
3. Adjacent to the button, enter the number of previous frames you want to see.

Saving DrawPlus Animations

- Choose **File>Save...**. DrawPlus saves animation documents in the proprietary .DPA format (Drawings are saved as .DPPs).

Previewing your animation

- Select **Preview Animation** from the Animation toolbar. The animation loads into the Preview window and begins playing at its actual size and speed. Notice that you see only the drawn portion of the animation—any extra surrounding white space is cropped away.

You can use the control buttons (Play, Stop, Back, and Forward) to review individual frames.

If you want to preview the animation in your Web browser, choose **Preview in Browser** from the File menu. This actually exports a *temporary* copy of the animation, using the current export settings (see below) and displays it in your Web browser. You can leave the browser open and DrawPlus will find it again next time you issue the command.

Adjusting animation properties

You can set the frame duration—how long each frame displays—both globally and locally, and set whether the animation plays as a continuous loop or repeats a certain number of times.

The **Export Optimizer** (see the previous topic) also lets you set the duration of individual frames and the loop or repeat playback mode.

To set a global frame duration (same timing for each frame):

1. Select **Animation Properties** from the Animation toolbar.
   OR
   Click the **Options** button at the top right of the Frames tab and select **Animation Properties...** from the menu.
2. Check the **Display each frame for** box and specify a duration setting in hundredths of a second.
3. Click **OK**.

Setting the frame timing globally in this way resets any individual frame timings you may have set. In general, set the global frame duration first, then go back and adjust individual frame timings as needed.

To set the duration of an individual frame:

1. Select the individual frame in the Frames tab.
2. Select **Frame Properties** from the Animation toolbar or via right-click in the Frames tab.
3. Specify a duration setting in the **Display frame for** box for the frame.

To specify loop or repeat playback:

1. Select **Animation Properties** from the Animation toolbar.
   OR
   Click the **Options** button at the top right of the Frames tab and select **Animation Properties...** from the menu.
2. Enable either **Loop continuously** (the default) or **Repeat animation for**, and set the number of repeats if needed.

Exporting your animation

1. Select **Export Animation** from the Animation toolbar.
   OR
   Click the **Options** button at the top right of the Frames tab and select **Export Animation...** from the menu.
   OR
   Choose **Export...** from the File menu.

   The **Export Optimizer** appears.
2. In the **Format** tab, select "Animated GIF" or "AVI" from the **Format** drop-down menu.
3. From the **Settings** tab, set a size for the animation and whether it is based on the whole page, selected regions or objects.
4. On the **Animation** tab, which only appears in Animation Mode, you can preview single frames or run the animation sequence, and make some final playback adjustments to the animation properties.
5. Click the **Export** button (or **Close** to simply record the settings if you plan to preview in a browser first).
6. Provide a file name and folder location, and click **Save**. Don't worry if you have extra white space around your image. Any unused border area will be cropped automatically, just as you saw in the Preview window.

Export formats

You can export to a variety of formats but typically for animations you will be picking the Animated GIF or AVI formats.

- **Animated GIF:** This default format (pre-selected) is what makes Web animation possible, for a couple of reasons. First, it's universally supported by Web browsers. Second, it's a multi-part format, capable of encoding not just one image but multiple images in the same file. A .GIF animation player or Web browser can display these images in sequence, in accordance with certain settings (looping, frame delay, etc.) included in the file. The result—it moves! For recommended export settings see Using the Export Optimizer on p. 222.

- **AVI** (Audio-Video Interleaved): This video format is commonly used on the Windows platform to encode image sequences in sync with a mono or stereo sound track. You can use DrawPlus to create title sequences and the like, then export them to the uncompressed .AVI format (without audio, of course) using 24-bit colour. If you intend to apply a **codec** (compression/decompression scheme) you can do so later, using a video editor. Note that .AVIs don't internally support certain playback properties of the animated .GIF format, such as "Endless Loop." Depending on which program you'll be using to play back the .AVI, however, you may be able to achieve these effects.

Animation Techniques

QuickShape Animation

The QuickShape flyout offers dozens of shapes, each with its own variations. The ease with which you can alter QuickShapes (using the Node Tool) makes them ideal starting points for geometric animation effects, whether used singly or in combination with text or other elements.

Remember that dragging the node handles of any QuickShape (see p. 104) provides an instant preview of many possible animation effects. By using this feature you can create frame sequences by cloning frames and adjusting the object as you go. Of course, you can vary the size and position of the QuickShape, too. In the example below, a Quick Clock shape can be animated by cloning each quickshape while changing the minute hand of the clock face.

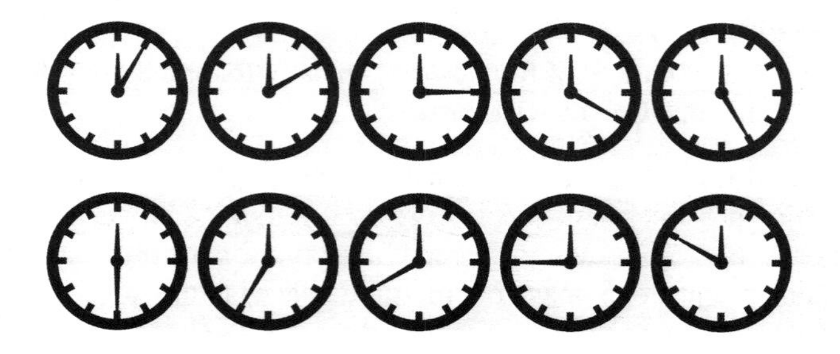

Text animation

So far we've dealt exclusively with QuickShape objects, but the same basic principles of positioning and timing apply to any object you want to animate, including text. As you may know from working with text in Chapters 6 and 9, DrawPlus gives you a wide choice of ways to vary text, ranging from simple size or fill changes to more complex effects like envelope distortions or blends. As with QuickShapes, any ways means by which you can vary an object's appearance can be put to good use in animation.

Almost any change you can apply to text has potential as the basis for an animation effect when it's extended over a series of frames. For example, you can reposition each letter with the Node Tool, creating animated bouncing text.

Bounce Bounce Bounce Bounce

Bounce Bounce Bounce Bounce

You can also...

- Vary the extent of transparency over text from frame to frame, producing a soft-edge wipe transition.
- Rotate text around its centre, corners or edge midpoints through 360°, while varying its size.
- Create a "flip" effect by vertically stretching and compressing text with respect to a central axis.
- Reduce or enlarge a text object as it moves toward a vanishing point.
- Employ curved text sequences that change over time.

Frame Edge Effects

To give the impression that some of your objects appear to float out of the frame you can use the edge of the page as your frame edge—cropping during export will ensure your animation is as you wished.

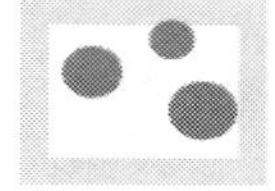

Perception effects

Grab a book on optical illusions, or explore the World Wide Web for perception demonstrations. Sometimes quite eye-catching effects are possible with very simple combinations of lines and shapes.

- The **Whirlpool** Illusion: A Quick Spiral, available as a preset QuickShape, can be modified frame by frame resulting in a swirling effect—useful when drawing washing machines, a moving propeller, or even plug holes.

- **The Barber Pole Illusion:** A variation on the above, using diagonal stripes moving up or down, creates the effect of a rotating pole. Try using more of an S-shape to suggest a convex pole. Turned sideways, it becomes a twisting screw or worm gear.

Character animation

The art of character animation is somewhat beyond the scope of this chapter. But by using supplied samples, clipart and applying the basic principles, you can get amusing and effective results. For example, a cartoon cat can be simply drawn to create a "walking" motion frame by frame:

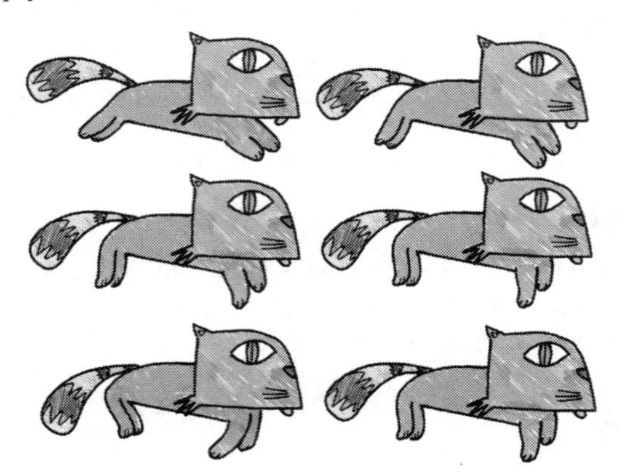

Remember to apply the concepts of stretching and squashing, overlapping frames for smooth movement, arc motion, and timing. Here are some other tips to keep in mind:

- **Anticipation:** You can set up a major action with a minor "get ready, get set" action. For example, before a frog leaps up into the air, it could squat down a bit. Subtle preparatory gestures like this add interest without adding a lot of extra frames.
- **Exaggeration:** In cartoons, virtually anything goes. Wild facial expressions, elastic arm and hand movements, and so on—just as long as the basic timing works.
- **Simplification:** Don't overdraw—take your cue from established cartoon conventions. There's probably a good reason why our favourite cartoon animals all seem to have only three fingers and a thumb!

Simulations

Realistic animations have a definite place in presentations and instructional materials. Whether you're demonstrating the beating of a heart, cog wheels turning, changes in a stock price, a route to follow on a map, or principles of basic physics, you can combine animated GIFs with HTML-based pages to deliver your message effectively.

- Consider using bitmaps as background frames and animating over them.
- Rather than trying to show too much or make too many points in one animation, break complex processes down into separate GIFs so each stage is conveyed clearly.
- Except for essential labels, place explanatory text and titles outside the animation to conserve file size.
- Scale file sizes to the delivery platform.

Web Graphics

For the most part, the budding artist will output their graphics to a home printer, electronically to a professional printing bureau (as a PDF) or as a graphic (either for inclusion in another program or as part of an Internet-accessible Web page). The export of your DrawPlus designs as graphics for the Web is covered later in Exporting graphics (p. 219).

Let's now take a look at how graphics intended for the Web environment can be made more intelligent and powerful by creation of clickable objects or regions prior to export. The remainder of this chapter describes the main tools for doing this—the **Image Slice Tool** and the hotspot tools, **Hotspot Rectangle, Hotspot Circle** and **Hotspot Polygon**.

Web image slicing

With **image slicing**, a graphic is carved up into smaller graphics—each of which can have its own link, like any Web graphic—and DrawPlus saves the sections as separate files when you export the image. The process also outputs HTML tags describing a table containing the separate image files, so that a Web browser can reassemble them seamlessly. The result appears as a single larger graphic, but with different regions linked to different targets.

The **Image Slice Tool** lets you subdivide the page into separate sections which can be exported using the .GIF, .JPG or .PNG format. For each rectangular slice object you draw, you can specify alternate text, URL links, and/or JavaScript rollover code. DrawPlus intelligently carves the page area into additional sections as needed, based on the slice objects you've specified.

Web hotspots

Whereas image slicing subdivides an entire graphic into smaller graphics and exports them separately, **hotspots** can be used to create "hot" (hyperlinked) regions (with associated URL target and/or alternate text) which are drawn over selected parts of an image—great for defining isolated and/or irregularly shaped clickable regions on a single Web graphic.

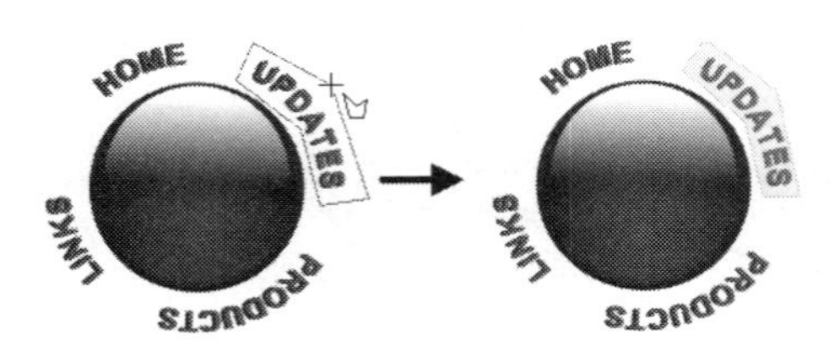

In the graphic, you see a detail of one quadrant of the graphic, showing a hotspot being drawn and then custom-shaped to fit the underlying text. Hotspots are especially useful on photographic images.

Note that hotspots aren't attached to a particular image, but become part of a larger "map" that gets exported along with an image in the form of HTML code. It's then up to the Web developer to embed the image map code properly into the Web page.

DrawPlus hotspots don't include JavaScript rollover capability.

Why use hotspots instead of slices? Use hotspots if you want to define isolated and/or irregularly shaped, clickable regions on a single Web graphic, as opposed to subdividing the entire graphic into rectangular image slices.

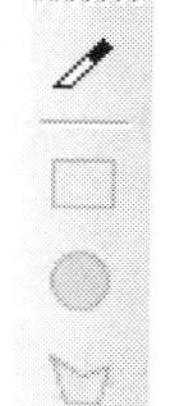

The **Web toolbar** hosts three tools (**Hotspot Rectangle**, **Hotspot Circle**, and **Hotspot Polygon**) for creating and editing hotspots.

You may need to switch the Web toolbar on via **View>Studio Tabs**.

Generally you draw the hotspots first, then go back to adjust their shape and add Web properties. Simply select the right tool for the job and draw your hotspot. (To draw a polygon, drag and release the mouse button to define each line segment; double-click to close the polygon.) The hotspot appears as a pink-shaded region.

Hotspots can be moved with the Pointer, Rotate or Node Tool—resize with the Pointer Tool or rotate with the Rotate Tool. You may need to click twice (and watch the HintLine) to be sure you've selected the hotspot and not another object in the same spot.

As with image slices, you specify each hotspot's hyperlink target (URL) and alternate text by double-clicking it (or right-clicking and choosing **Properties...**), then entering the information in the dialog.

To preview the graphic in your Web browser or do a final export, follow the steps described above for image slices. First, make sure that the **Hotspots** box on the Settings tab of the Export Optimizer is checked. The output will consist of one image file (for example, MYFILE.JPG) and one HTML file (for example, MYFILE.HTML). The HTML file contains the hotspot description, ready to be pasted into the source code for the Web page.

JavaScript Rollovers

Even if you don't have a clue what "JavaScript Rollovers" are, you've probably seen them in action. You've pointed your mouse at a graphic (such as a navigation bar button) on a Web page, and seen it instantly change colour or become a different picture. That's what JavaScript rollovers can accomplish.

The term **rollover** refers to an interaction between a mouse and a screen graphic. When you point to a Web page graphic, your mouse pointer physically enters the screen region occupied by the graphic. This triggers an **event** called a "mouseover" and, if the underlying code is there to "trap" this event, it can trigger some other event—such as displaying another graphic at the same location. In other words, the **state** of the graphic changes in response to screen events.

DrawPlus gives you the option of adding rollover responses to image slice objects. The necessary JavaScript code is generated automatically. There are four basic steps:

1. Divide the image into slice objects.
2. Specify which rollover states you want to activate for each slice object by checking boxes in each object's Properties dialog.
3. Create the alternate graphics for each state. (It will help to understand the basics of DrawPlus layers as described on p. 171.)
4. Preview in a browser, revise as needed, and then export.

For more information see DrawPlus help (search "rollover" in the Index) for additional pointers—for example, how rollover layers differ somewhat from standard layers, and how to create a document that uses one or more additional standard layers as a background for your rollover states.

Tutorial Resources

For more experience with the tools and techniques covered in this chapter, we recommend these PDF-based tutorials (go to **Help>Tutorials** in DrawPlus):

Try this tutorial...	For practice with these tools and techniques...
Create an Animated Cartoon	Animation features, Clone Frame, Export Animation
Blend and Animate Objects	Animation features, Morphing between Objects, Animation Previews
Create Filter Effects	Convert to Animation
Create Web Button Rollovers	Creating Web buttons, Making Rollovers, Rollover States, Hotspots and slices, Export Optimizer
Add Perspective to a Web button/ Create Raised and Sunken Buttons	Creating Web Buttons

Jump between your PDF tutorials and DrawPlus with **Alt-Tab**.

11
Exporting and Publishing

Exporting graphics

Whether you're producing pictures for the Web or the printed page, in order to use a DrawPlus drawing in another program you'll need to **export** it to one of the many standard graphics formats DrawPlus supports. Especially if you're exporting Web bitmap images, you'll want to read the following sections and take advantage of the Export Optimizer, which will greatly help you in reducing file sizes as far as possible while maintaining image quality.

In order to grasp what "optimization"—the aforementioned tradeoff between file size and image quality—is all about, it's useful to understand the difference between **draw** or **vector** graphics, like those created by DrawPlus, and **bitmap** images (including .BMPs, .GIFs, and .JPGs), also known as **paint** or **raster** images. Whereas draw graphics are resolution-independent and use commands such as "draw a line from A to B," bitmaps are built from a matrix of dots ("pixels"), rather like the squares on a sheet of graph paper.

Bitmaps

Technically speaking, a bitmap is basically a "map" of numbers that tell each pixel on a computer monitor what colour it should be. And since computer numbers consist of binary digits (1's and 0's, or "bits"), each pixel in effect has one or more bits backing it up, telling it what to do. From this fact arises the concept of **bit depth** (also known as "pixel depth"), one of the essential attributes of any bitmap image. Bitmaps not only have height and width, they have depth. The more bits assigned to each pixel, the more possible colour states the pixel can be told to take—the greater its "colour depth."

For example: If you're only using 1 bit per pixel, the pixel can only be ON or OFF, in other words "1" or "0," the two states of the bit—hence white or black (**monochrome**). By comparison, a bit depth of 4 bits per pixel can store 16 values; 8 bits per pixel, 256, and so on. 16-bit images have roughly "thousands" of values to describe each pixel's colour, and 24-bit images have "millions." Not surprisingly, the file size of an image is basically the product of its linear dimensions (number of pixels) times its bit depth, so a picture (perhaps of a heart) saved as a 24-bit image would take up three times as much disk space as an 8-bit version.

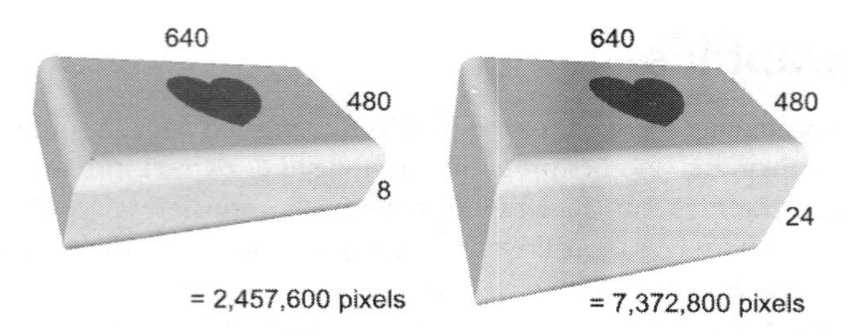

While file size is still an issue—even though hard disk capacity and cost have improved dramatically, the Export Optimizer still seeks to offer you as optimum a file size as possible for your chosen exported graphic format.

For the Web, several graphics formats have emerged as standards—and the following descriptions, along with details on Export Optimizer options, will help you make informed choices at export time.

Remember that the default settings of the Export Optimizer are intended for web graphics export, in particular, the resolution is set to 96 dpi (the standard screen resolution for Windows).

Web file formats

Three of the principal file formats used for Web pictures and animation are .GIF, .JPG, and .PNG. Let's look at each in turn.

- The **.GIF (Graphics Interchange Format)** file format is universally supported in Web browsers for both static and animated Web graphics. It's a **lossless** format (there's no image degradation) with excellent compression but a limitation of 256 colours. Use it for non-photographic images with sharp edges and geometrics—for example buttons, bursts, decorative elements, and text graphics. It's suitable for greyscale photos as well. Blurred shadows, anti-aliased edges, and subtle transparency effects, however, don't survive so well. Pixels that aren't 100% transparent will end up opaque, and the exported graphic will display sharp or even ragged edges when viewed over a Web page background.

  The .GIF format supports binary transparency. That is, any portion of the image may be either fully opaque or fully transparent. Typically, this is used to eliminate the box-shaped frame around the graphic that would otherwise be present. Elements with rounded edges, such as characters or shapes, preserve their contours over any background colour or pattern.

  GIF is also a *multi-part* format, which means one file can store multiple images. As such, it's the preferred format for Web animations (see earlier in this chapter).

- The **.JPG** or **JPEG (Joint Photographic Experts Group)** file format, like .GIF, is universally supported in Web browsers. Unlike .GIF, it encodes 24-bit images and is a **lossy** format (i.e., it discards some image information) with variable compression settings. JPG is clearly the format of choice for full-colour onscreen illustrations or photographic images. For "black and white" (really 256-level, 8-bit greyscale) photos, it has no particular advantages over .GIF.

  When exporting as a JPG, you can use a slider to choose one setting from 10 possible levels. At one end of the scale, the export applies maximum compression and produces an extremely small (but quite ugly) image. At the other end, there is effectively no loss of quality, but file sizes are relatively much larger, although still compact compared to BMPs, for example.

  When choosing a quality setting for .JPG export, keep in mind the number of times you expect to be re-exporting a particular image. A photograph may look fine in the Export Optimizer the first time you export it at .JPG level 6, but after several such saves, you'll really see a cumulative quality loss.

- For Web graphics, the newer **.PNG (Portable Network Graphics)**, pronounced "ping," format has a number of advantages over .GIF—the main ones, from an artist's perspective, being "lossless" 24-bit images and support for variable transparency. Whereas .GIF supports simple binary ("on-off") transparency, .PNG allows up to 254 levels of partial transparency for normal images. The image file includes an "alpha channel" that directs pixels in the foreground image to merge with those in a background image. Most commonly used with 24-bit images, anti-aliasing creates the illusion of smooth curves by varying pixel colours-—for rounded images that look good against any background, not just against a white background. It's especially useful for the small graphics commonly used on Web pages, such as bullets and fancy text.

Using the Export Optimizer

The **Export Optimizer** appears when you choose **Export** from the File menu. It consists of a left-hand options region and a right-hand preview display, with additional buttons along the bottom of the dialog. Two tabs appear in Drawing Mode, and a third for animation export (as discussed in the previous chapter).

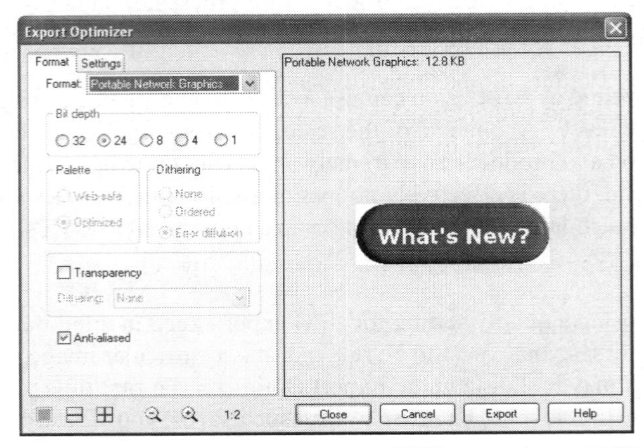

To change the display scale, click the **Zoom In** or **Zoom Out** buttons on the bottom row (the above button has been zoomed out by 50%). When zoomed in, you can also pan around different portions of the image, by dragging the hand cursor (along with the image) around the preview pane.

To adjust the preview display, click one of the View buttons at the lower left to select **Single**, **Double**, or **Quad** display. The illustration above shows Single view. The multi-pane (Double and Quad) settings let you compare different export settings for one or more file formats. Just click one of the display panes to select it as the active pane, then choose an export format from the list and specific options for the format. Each time you make a new choice, the active pane updates to show the effect of filtering using the new settings, as well as the estimated file size!

On the **Settings** tab, you can scale the image to a new size if desired, or adjust the dpi (dots per inch) setting. For graphics to be used onscreen (e.g., web graphics), it's best to leave these values intact.

When you've decided on the optimum export settings, click the dialog's **Export** button to proceed with the actual exporting. If you click **Close**, DrawPlus remembers your preferred format and settings, particularly useful for adjusting the GIF setting which are used if you preview the image in a browser (using **File>Preview in Browser**).

To optimize your use of the Export Optimizer, so to speak, here's a rundown of some of the terminology used on the Format tab and some suggested guidelines (focused on the JPG and PNG formats):

- **Bit Depth:** Bit depth relates to the number of colours in the exported image. In general, images with higher bit depth take up more disk space. Choose the bit depth that corresponds to the number of colours in the exported image. **32-bit** and **24-bit** settings preserve full colour; 32-bit includes 8 extra bits for an alpha (transparency) channel and is equivalent to choosing 24-bit with Transparency switched on. **8-bit** (256 colours) is the only available setting for animations, and the maximum supported by the format.

- **Transparency: GIF** files support single-level (on/off) transparency, so if you check **Transparency** and export as a GIF, any "checkerboard" regions of your graphic (those with no pixels or 0% opacity) will turn into transparent regions in the GIF; all other regions will become opaque. When exporting as a full-colour **PNG**, full gradations of transparency in your original design are preserved. (See details on each format above.) DrawPlus also provides **Dithering** options (for GIFs and 8-bit-or-less PNGs) which are similar to those for image colours (see DrawPlus help). Dithering in regions of partial transparency causes certain pixels to drop out in a patterned way. These tiny dropouts allow underlying colours to show through, achieving smoother blends in these regions despite the limitation of single-level transparency.

- **Anti-aliasing**: Leave **Anti-aliased** checked to preserve edge smoothness, or uncheck the box for sharp edges, which are sometimes desirable.

- **Quality:** With the .JPG format, recommended for photographic backgrounds, you can set the level of **Quality** desired using a slider. As you might expect, the highest-quality setting uses least compression, with no loss of image quality but the largest file size. The lowest-quality setting applies maximum compression for smallest size, but yields rather poor quality.

There are other export options available via the Settings tab, all differing depending on the type of graphic to be exported. See DrawPlus help for full details of each setting.

Publishing via PDF or Print

DrawPlus supports scaling, tiling, colour separations, and many other useful printing options. Here we'll cover what you need to know for basic desktop printer output. If you're working with a service bureau or professional printer and need to provide PDF or PostScript output, see p. 227 or DrawPlus help, respectively.

To print to your desktop printer:

- Click the **Print** button on the Standard toolbar.

The Print dialog appears.

To print:

1. On the **General** tab, select a printer from the list. If necessary, click the **Properties** button to set up the printer for the correct orientation and page order. Set the page size from the **Advanced** button.
2. If necessary, click the **Layout** tab to set special print options such as scaling, thumbnails, multiple pages, or tiling. For details, see Printing Special Formats on p. 225.
3. Select the print range to be printed—choose the whole document, current page, selected pages/page ranges as options.
4. Select the number of copies.
5. If required, save the current settings to a Print profile (see p. 228).

The Preview window shows how your drawing maps to the selected paper size. You can click the dialog's **Preview** button to hide/show the window.

Previewing the Printed Page

The **Print Preview** mode changes the screen view to display your layout without frames, guides, rulers, and other screen items.

1. Click the **Print Preview** button on the Standard toolbar.

In Print Preview mode, the lower toolbar provides a variety of familiar view options, such as zoom in/out, zoom to a selected area, fit to page or to actual size.

2. Click the **Close** button to exit from Print Preview.

Printing Special Formats

Printing booklets

DrawPlus automatically performs **imposition** of folded documents when you use **File>Page Setup...** and select a **Booklet** document type. The settings ensure that two or four pages of the drawing are printed on each sheet of paper, with pages printed following the booklet sequence. This saves you from having to calculate how to position and collate pairs of pages on a single larger page, and lets you use automatic page numbering for the booklet pages.

To produce double-sided sheets, use your printer's double-sided option or run sheets through twice, printing first the front and then the back of the sheet (reverse top and bottom between runs). The sheets can then be collated and bound at their centre to produce a booklet, with all the pages in the correct sequence.

Printing special folded documents

DrawPlus also performs **imposition** of other more unusual document types when you use **File>Page Setup...** and select a **Special Folded** document type. The types, most appropriate to invitations and greeting cards, include Tent Card, and Side/Top Fold Menu, Quarter size, Tri-Fold, or Z-Fold.

Printing posters and banners

Posters and banners are large-format documents where the page size extends across multiple sheets of paper. To have DrawPlus take care of the printing, set up your drawing beforehand using **File>Page Setup...** (with the **Large** document type option) to preview and select a particular preset arrangement.

Even if the drawing isn't set up as a poster or banner, you can use tiling and scaling settings (see "Scaling" and "Tiling" below) to print onto multiple sheets from a standard size page. Each section or tile is printed on a single sheet of paper, and the various tiles can then be joined to form the complete page.

Scaling

- Under "Special Printing" on the Print dialog's **Layout** tab, set the "As in document - % Scale factor" option to specify a custom scaling percentage. The default is 100% or normal size. To scale your work to be printed at a larger size, specify a larger value; to scale down, specify a smaller value. Check **Fit Many** to have DrawPlus fit as many pages as possible on each sheet—for example, two A5 pages on a landscape A4 sheet.

- Set "Scale to fit paper size" values to adjust artwork automatically to fit neatly on the printed page.
- Note that the Fit Many option ignores printer margins, while Scale to Fit takes them into account. So if you use Fit Many, make sure your page layout borders don't extend beyond the printable region.

Printing business cards and labels

While DrawPlus can deal with Large format documents it is equally suited to documents where the design can be repeated multiple times on the same page during printing. Set up your drawing beforehand using **File>Page Setup...** (with the **Small** document type option) to preview and select a particular preset arrangement.

At print time, you can set the "Multiple pages per sheet" option to **Repeat pages to fill sheet**, **Repeat pages by N times** or **Full sheet of each page** in the **Print>Layout** tab. You can tell DrawPlus to skip a certain number of regions on the first sheet of paper—useful if, for example, you've already peeled off several labels from a label sheet, and don't want to print on the peeled-off sections. Check the Preview window to see how the output will look.

If you haven't set up the drawing as a Small Drawing, but still want to print multiple pages per sheet, try using the **Fit Many** option (see "Scaling" above). Note that this option ignores printer margins and doesn't change the imposition (orientation) of output pages.

Printing thumbnails

- Under "Special Printing" on the Print dialog's **Layout** tab, set the **Print as thumbnails** option to print multiple pages at a reduced size on each printed sheet, taking printer margins into account. Specify the number of thumbnails per sheet in the value box.

DrawPlus will print each page of the drawing at a reduced size, with the specified number of small pages or "thumbnails" neatly positioned on each printed sheet.

Tiling

- Under "Tiling" on the Print dialog's **Layout** tab, check the **Print tiled pages** option to print large (or enlarged) pages using multiple sheets of paper.
- Set the **% Scale factor** to print at a larger size (e.g. 300%)

Each section or tile is printed on a single sheet of paper; the various tiles can then be joined to form the complete page. Use this option for printing at larger sizes than the maximum paper size of your printer, typically for creating banners and posters. To simplify arrangement of the tiles and to allow for printer margins, you can specify a **Tile overlap** value.

Generating Professional Output

Beyond printing your own copies on a desktop printer, or having copies photo-reproduced at a quick print shop, you may wish to consider professional (typically offset) printing. For example, if you need to reproduce more than about 500 copies of a piece, photocopying begins to lose its economic advantages. Or you may need **spot colour** or **process colour** printing for a particular job. You can output your DrawPlus drawing and hand it off to any trusted commercial printer.

Unless you're handing off camera-ready artwork, your print provider will specify the format in which you should submit the drawing: either **PDF/X** or **PostScript** (see DrawPlus Help). Once you've decided whether to output as PDF or PostScript, you'll need to set Prepress options before choosing the appropriate output command.

The Separation and Pre-press options are further described in the DrawPlus Help. In addition, the process for producing colour separations is detailed.

PDF/X

PDF (short for Portable Document Format) is a cross-platform format developed by Adobe to handle documents in a device- and platform-independent manner. PDF excels as an electronic distribution medium and the reliable **PDF/X** formats are perfect for delivering a drawing file to a professional printer. In recent years, print shops are moving away from PostScript and toward the newer, more reliable **PDF/X** formats expressly targeted for graphic arts and high quality reproduction. Your print partner can tell you whether to deliver PDF/X-1 or PDF/X-1a (DrawPlus supports both)—but from the DrawPlus end of things you won't see a difference. In either mode, all your drawing's colours will be output in the CMYK colour space, and fonts you've used will be embedded. A single PDF/X file will contain all the necessary information (fonts, images, graphics, and text) your print partner requires to generate either spot or process colour separations.

To output a drawing as a PDF/X file:

1. Choose **Publish as PDF…** from the File menu.
2. Review General and Advanced tab settings (see DrawPlus Help for more details).

- When preparing a PDF/X file for professional printing, choose either "PDF X/1" or "PDF X/1a" in the General tab's **Compatibility** drop-down list, as advised by your print partner. Also inquire whether or not to **Impose pages**; this option is fine for desktop printing of a folded drawing or one that uses facing pages, but a professional printer may prefer you to leave the imposition (page sequencing) to them.

3. Review Prepress tab settings.

If you checked **Preview PDF file in Acrobat**, the resulting PDF file appears in the version of Adobe Acrobat Reader installed on your system.

Saving Print Profiles

You can save the current combination of settings made in the Print dialog as a **print profile** with a unique name. Note that the profile includes settings from all tabs except the Separations tab. (By the way, don't confuse these DrawPlus "print profiles" with ICC "device profiles.")

To save current print settings as a print profile:

- On the Print dialog's **General** tab, click the **Save As...** button next to the Print Profile list.
- Type in a new name and click **OK**.

The settings are saved as a file with the extension .PPR.

You can restore the profile later on simply by choosing its name in the list.

Tutorial Resources

For more experience with the tools and techniques covered in this chapter, we recommend these PDF-based tutorials (go to **Help>Tutorials** in DrawPlus):

Try this tutorial...	For practice with these tools and techniques...
Design a Cartoon Character Movie Poster	Printing

Jump between your PDF tutorials and DrawPlus with **Alt-Tab**.

Index

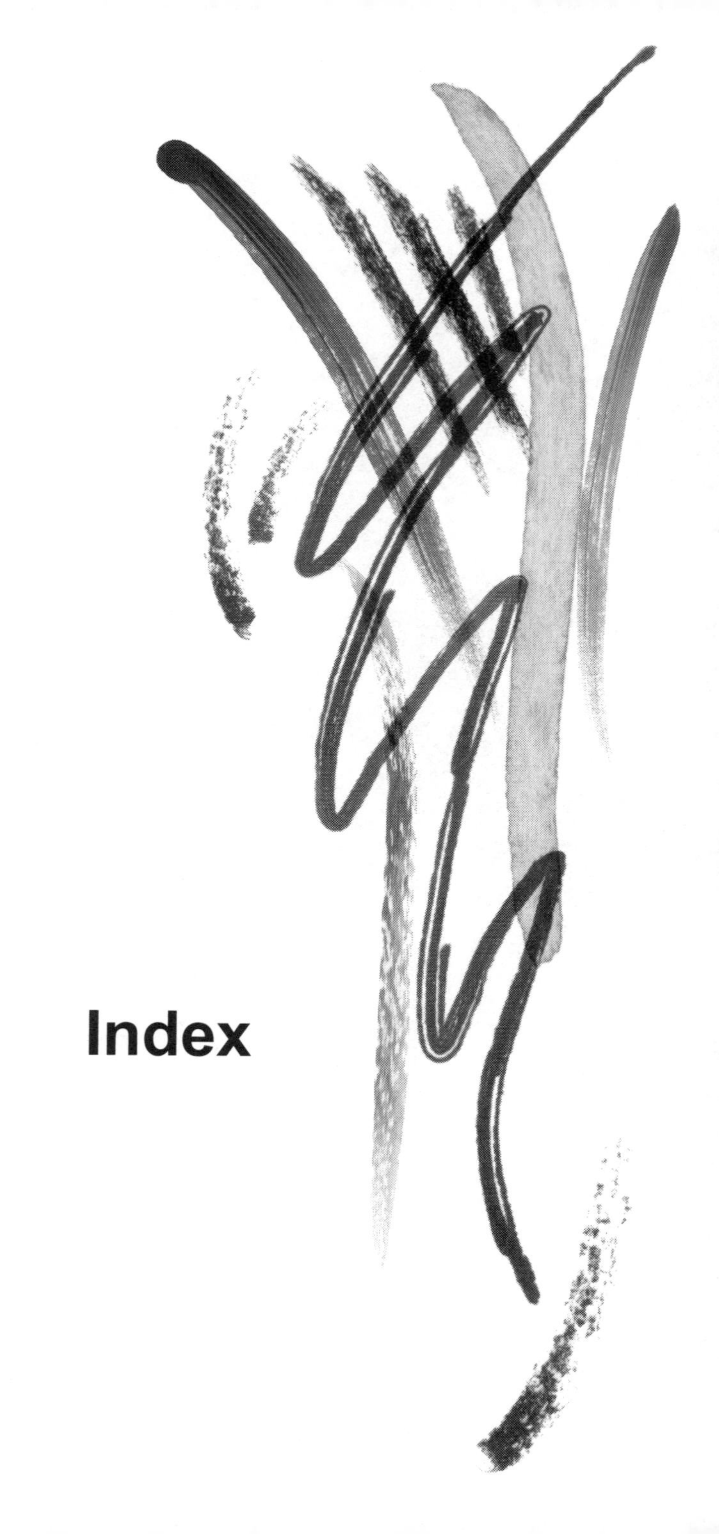